FROM ITALY & BACK
COMING FULL CIRCLE

Rediscovering Our Roots

ANN VOTTA

Copyrighted Material

From Italy and Back: Coming Full Circle
Rediscovering Our Roots
Ann Votta

Copyright © 2018 by AV Publishing LLC.
All Rights Reserved.

No part of this publication may be reproduced, stored in a retrieval system or transmitted, in any form or by any means—electronic, mechanical, photocopying, recording or otherwise—without prior written permission from the publisher, except for the inclusion of brief quotations in a review.

For information about this title or to order other books and/or electronic media, contact the publisher:

AV Publishing LLC
1176 Tahiti Parkway
Sarasota, FL 34236
AV Publishers.com
508-221-8650

Library of Congress Control Number: 2018942461

ISBNs:
978-0-9889757-3-6 Print
978-0-98897574-3 eBook

Printed in the United States of America

Cover and Interior design: 1106 Design

Cover Photo: Adelina DelZio Marano (Grandma), Mary Marano Preston (Aunt Mary), Mauretta DelZio Marano (Zizi), and Helen Marano Patavino (Mom) on Grandma's lap. c. 1915.

Publisher's Cataloging-In-Publication Data
(Prepared by The Donohue Group, Inc.)

Names: Votta, Ann.
Title: From Italy & back : coming full circle : rediscovering our roots / Ann Votta.
Other Titles: From Italy and back
Description: Sarasota, FL : AV Publishing LLC, [2018]
Identifiers: ISBN 9780988975736 | ISBN 9780988975743 (ebook)
Subjects: LCSH: Votta, Ann--Travel--Italy. | Votta, Ann--Family. | Italian Americans--Biography. | Italy--Genealogy. | LCGFT: Autobiographies.
Classification: LCC E184.I8 V68 2018 (print) | LCC E184.I8 (ebook) | DDC 973/.0451/0092--dc23

Dedicated to our grandparents, Adelina and Antonio Marano; Anna Maria and Michele Patavino; and Guiseppe Votta.

They had the courage to leave Italy for a better life in America. They left us with the desire to go back.

Also by Ann Votta:

Reunited: When the Past Becomes a Present

Acknowledgments

This project has been in the works for a long time. I never thought it would take more than five years to complete, but with so many starts and stops, no wonder I have been at it so long.

There would be no book or anything to tell at all if it weren't for the courage and strength and perseverance of our grandparents who left their tiny villages in the regions of Molise and Puglia in Italy so long ago to seek a better life in America. They faced many challenges and struggles. Their unique experiences during their lifetime provided me with the blessed life I have enjoyed. I am indebted to them for that.

Writing this book has also given me a much deeper respect for my exceptional parents, Helen and Carmen Patavino; for the loving and nurturing environment they created for my sister Emma and me in which to grow and thrive. I miss their strength and encouragement every day—and their laughter.

Thanks also to my husband, Alan Votta, for sticking with me through the stops and starts and for expecting me to carry on and finish it. His diary entries from our trips to Italy in 2010 and 2012 are indicative of his attention to detail and his beautiful spirit and *joi de vivre*. Alan also spent many hours re-reading and editing the manuscript with me and offered suggestions for improvement along the way.

My sister, Emma Patavino Migdal, read through early copies of the manuscript and offered much by helping me remember some things and events from our childhood that were no longer memories of mine. Because of the four-year difference in our ages, we recollected some things differently. Her additions to my story gave depth and freshness. And we had fun reminiscing and laughing about what we agreed was a most idyllic childhood.

My Italian cousin, Piera Fogliato from Torino, Italy, deserves gratitude as well for her devotion to her American relatives, her promise to her grandmother, Amalia Marano, to learn English, and her continued love for all of us. I have noted her contributions to our Italian life throughout the book.

Thanks also must go to Peter Farina and his staff from *Italy Mondo*, the folks who assisted us on our journey to secure our Italian citizenship. We started the process not long after Peter established his company in New York to help Italian-Americans research their heritage and become citizens of Italy. In fact we were even considered his "guinea pigs" (no pun intended) by traveling to Italy and establishing residency to start the process over there. We love the fact that we hold two passports—American and Italian.

Lastly, I could not have completed writing this without the help I received from my daughter, Leigh Vincola. She became mentor, editor, and general supporter during the entire process.

ACKNOWLEDGMENTS

Her own connection to Italy gave us the impetus to begin the search for our roots and the desire to find out more. It was her research that led us to *Italy Mondo* and eventual dual citizenship for all of us. Leigh lived and worked in Italy for more than two years. Having her there made our last two trips to Italy such magnificent events. Without her, we never would have seen or done the many wonderful things that made those trips so extra special. I am so proud of all of her accomplishments and I am grateful that I raised a daughter who became fascinated with her heritage and wanted to live as an Italian.

Writing this book is in loving memory of my grandparents and my parents and my aunts, uncles, and cousins who have passed on. Since I am now the eldest living Marano relative, it is my hope that I have brought back fond memories to my cousins so that they can relay some of these stories to their children and grandchildren and keep those treasures alive.

The journey doesn't end. We look forward to what lies ahead and continuing with the back-and-forth.

Contents

Acknowledgments	vii
Introduction	xiii

PART ONE
Childhood Memories

1	Background	3
2	La Famiglia	11
3	Buon Natale et Buona Pasqua	45
4	Quatiere	51
5	Paternal Grandparents	63
6	Growing Up Italian-American	73

PART TWO
Travels in Italy

1	Overview	79
2	First Trip: 1967	83
3	Deepening the Love of a Country	95
4	Finding Our Roots	105
5	Italy with Alan	113

PART THREE
Our Connection to the Country of Our Ancestors

1 Becoming Italian Citizens 119
2 Cultural Differences Between Italians
  and Americans 125

Afterword

Alan's Diary Entries from 2010 and 2012 131
About the Author 183

Introduction

I was born in Mount Vernon, New York, and most of my childhood was spent in Yonkers, New York. My mother was born in Mount Vernon, New York, and my father was born in the Bronx, New York. My grandparents—on both my mother and father's side—spent the early part of their lives in the south of Italy—in Molise and Puglia.

I love New York and I love America. And I love Italy—the country of my ancestors.

As my life has progressed (now that I have lived three quarters of a century) I appreciate my Italian heritage more and more every day. My numerous trips to the country my ancestors left many years ago have doubtless contributed to that appreciation. In 2012 I became an Italian citizen after my husband, my daughter, and I applied for citizenship. We each have two passports—American and Italian. I like to think my Italian passport somehow elevates my connection to my rich and vibrant heritage.

Both sets of my grandparents came to America at the beginning of the last century—more than 100 years ago. They left their homeland searching for a better life in America, and consequently they created a better life for me and for the rest of my family. Generally, life is quite different today in Italy than it was for them when they immigrated to the United States, but the cultural warmth and beauty of the land is still there in abundance. I have visited many of Italy's beautiful cities, provinces, and regions over the years and I feel that I know the country to some degree. The food, the wine, the people, the art, the history, the countryside, the sea, the lakes—who can argue that it is the BEST—especially the food, the wine and the PEOPLE!

My husband Alan and I agree that our Italian heritage plays an intrinsic role in our individual lives and in our life together. We feel a powerful pull toward the country of our ancestors. Nowadays many people are drawn to Ancestry.com and other Internet sites to begin researching their heritage and studying their DNA. Knowledge of one's genetic history and genealogy is very compelling, and we have fully embraced it. I have not had my DNA analyzed as of yet since I believe I know what it will tell me—i.e., that my roots are all from southern Europe.

My purpose here is to convey what it was like growing up in the 1940s and 1950s in an Italian-American family—a close and loving extended family—and how that contributed so much to who I am today. I also want to recreate and reminisce about some of the memorable experiences I enjoyed while traveling in Italy, which undoubtedly enhanced my love of this beautiful country.

Alan's grandfather, Giuseppe Votta, was born in Venafro, Italy, which is in the same region of Molise, where my paternal grandparents were born. Alan was able to apply for his Italian passport through his grandfather's lineage. Giuseppe Votta immigrated to Scotland and married there before finally settling in Yonkers, New York. Alan's heritage is mixed with Austrian, Scotch, and Hungarian thrown in there. His childhood was different than mine because of the multi-cultural influences on his life, not only Italian like mine.

The process of applying for Italian citizenship was indeed a fascinating endeavor with its many ups and downs, comical holdups, and overall frustrations, but the final outcome has been so worthwhile.

This is not a travel book. Although I have described many magnificent and beautiful spots in the country I love, it is not my intent to entice anyone to take a trip. It is, however, a testament to how much our cultural heritage impacts our lives and how I have embraced it fully.

Everyone loves Italy—no matter what one's ethnic background. And Italy is generally the trip of a lifetime for any traveler. For me, Italy represents so much more. It is what makes me, ME.

PART ONE

Childhood Memories

Background

I feel that I am fortunate to have Italian blood in my veins and I am certain that my heritage has provided me with a healthy constitution and good genes. My father and my mother

c. 1930, Marano family (maternal grandparents)

lived to ninety-two and ninety-nine respectively, and I assume that I still have some good years ahead of me. I also feel exceedingly fortunate and lucky to have grown up in an Italian-American household amid loving parents, grandparents, and relatives who contributed to my very happy childhood.

Although my upbringing was within an Italian environment, ours may not have been the stereotypical Italian environment that is sometimes depicted in the media and in film. My grandparents were immigrants; however, there was an element to their lifestyle that incorporated everything Italian, yet embraced what being American meant.

My grandfather, Antonio Marano, and his older brother, Pasquale Marano, were the first of the family to arrive in America. As skilled tradesmen they were not among the hundreds of thousands of Italians that made up the unskilled-labor market in the early part of the last century. They assimilated faster into their new culture than some of their counterparts and rose more quickly because of their trades. The immigrant community relied on their own strategies for survival and success in their new home, and for Italians that rested on two pillars—work and family. Their work provided an economic foothold in American society, which enabled them to provide for their families.

As part of the first generation born in this country, my mother and father made sure that they provided the very best for their family, i.e., what they could afford. They instilled a sense of achievement into my sister and me, with education most prominent. Dad finished only the eighth grade because he needed to go to work to help support his family. My mother graduated from high school and would have loved, beyond all measure, to attend college, but she, too, needed to go to work to bring that paycheck into the household.

I was born in 1943. Both sets of my grandparents emigrated from Italy between 1903 and 1910. After coming through Ellis Island in New York City, my maternal grandparents settled in Mount Vernon, New York, a suburb north of Manhattan, in what was then a very Italian enclave, and my paternal grandparents settled in the Bronx, New York, later moving to Mount Vernon.

Although my mother and my father were both born in the United States, not long after their parents arrived in America, they each had elder siblings who were born in the old country. They were part of the generation which straddled two cultures—born on one continent and making a new life in another. My mother stressed to us that my grandparents wanted their children to assimilate fully into American culture and although Italian

Grandma on a Sunday stroll with her daughters, c. 1920

was the language at home, she and her siblings were encouraged to speak only English outside of the house and even at home. The family enjoyed their life in America and adapted and changed in as many ways as they could, but yet held on to family traditions that were so important within Italian culture.

It was a different time. Immigrants were looked upon as outsiders, and Italian immigrants were considered the bottom of the barrel. Drawing attention to the differences of their American counterparts—especially in regard to language—was to be avoided. As a child my mother was exposed to the Italian language and heard it every day. She even spoke some Italian. But over her lifetime she forgot it. Years later, in her eighties, she took several courses to relearn Italian. (I am trying very hard—intermittingly, I admit—to learn Italian too, but it is HARD. Although I feel I have an ear for the language because I lived among the folks who spoke it when I was a child, I find that speaking Italian is another thing altogether and I am very timid about it.)

I was the eldest grandchild. My mother, father, baby sister, and I moved to the basement apartment of my grandmother's house when I was four years old. My father served in the Army during World War II. He was drafted when I was about six months old. There was no deferment for married men with children as the Second World War was winding down. After completing basic training in Mississippi, Dad was shipped to Germany and he served the remainder of his tour of duty in Germany until the war was over. My mother and I remained in the apartment where my parents lived after they were married. In 1945 when I was two years old and when Dad returned home from Germany,

BACKGROUND

Mom, Dad, Emmie and I in front of house on High Street

affordable housing for GIs was scarce, and besides that, the apartment we had been living in became unavailable. The landlord gave the apartment to his son who was also returning from the war. We needed to find a place to live.

Fortunately, there was an unfinished basement at my mother's family home on North High Street in Mount Vernon, New York. My father and several of my uncles (each of whom had the necessary expertise as plumbers and skilled laborers) worked hard to renovate the basement to make it livable for our little family, which by then included my sister Emma who was born in 1946.

Mom and I making bed in our basement apartment

We lived there until I was nine years old—when my parents had saved enough money (which included the $200 in my own bank account) to buy our house in Yonkers, New York. My sister remembers that my mother told her that Emmie and I "owned the front door" of our house in Yonkers.

My earliest childhood memories consisted of what happened in and around the house on North High Street, Mount Vernon, New York—with my maternal grandparents, great aunt and uncle, aunts, uncles, and cousins. Ours was a close family typical of the Italian-American life of the time.

La Famiglia

Grandpa and Zi Pasquale

The story begins with Grandpa and Zi Pasquale.

My grandfather, Antonio Marano, and his brother, Pasquale Marano, left Melfi, Italy, in the southern region of Puglia, in 1909 and arrived in Mount Vernon, New York. I do not know why Mount Vernon became their home. To my knowledge there were no other relatives or family friends living there prior to their arrival. Immigrants usually found a home in their new country where relatives had settled before them. After the two brothers established themselves in America and found a home and secured jobs, they sent for their wives—two sisters, Adelina DelZio and Mauretta DelZio. My Aunt Mary was a year old at the time and she traveled with Grandma and Zizi as they crossed the Atlantic to their new life in America.

Zi Pasquale was a skilled stonemason and as a result of his trade he was able to purchase the house on North High Street in

Mount Vernon, New York—a giant step toward realizing their American dream. That house, a two-story with a brick façade, became the family homestead until the 1990s and the focal point for all of my aunts, uncles and cousins. In fact, after we moved out of the basement of that house, other family members moved in and the house remained a lifesaver during hard times for the extended family.

My grandfather was an optician. He was employed by several optical companies in New York City as a younger man and then set up his own practice at home. The sign that read "Anthony T. Marano, Optician" hung on the house at 326 North High Street, Mount Vernon, New York. His fascinating display case of eyeglass lenses and his huge desk were prominent pieces in the living room. Grandpa fitted all of us for eyeglasses and made glasses for us whenever the need arose. Within the Italian community, it seemed there was always some family member who could provide a needed service when necessary. Because they owned their home and they were semi-professional and tradesmen, I guess you might say that they were more middle-class Italians than some immigrants of the time. And the lifestyle of the entire family contributed to that status.

Grandpa was very formal—and also very distant. He wore a three-piece suit every day—weekdays and on the weekend. I don't think I ever saw him without a jacket—maybe on the hottest of summer days when we went on family picnics to Sherwood Island in Westport, Connecticut, which was an annual event.

And Grandpa took a long walk, his constitutional or *passegiatta*, each day with his Stetson hat atop his head. He cut a distinguished figure in his suit with his ever-present watch fob visible.

LA FAMIGLIA

Formal picture of Grandma and Grandpa, c. 1930

Grandpa's reserved nature and stoic personality did not encourage a close relationship with him. We didn't sit on his lap or cuddle up with him like other affectionate Italian grandfathers.

Grandma and Grandpa at family picnic at Sherwood Island, c. 1950

Our Grandpa wasn't that kind of Grandpa, although there is one picture of Grandpa and me on the steps of the house when I was about a year old that belied that image. And by the way, our grandparents were always "Grandma and Grandpa" to us, never "*Nonna* or *Nonno*." I never learned those Italian words.

In 1967 Grandpa and I shared a greater connection as I began to plan my upcoming European trip, because I was going to visit his sister and her family in Torino, Italy. He hadn't seen the family members he'd left behind in Italy in more than

50 years. Grandpa and I sat together reading letters from the relatives and planning my visit. It was the one time in my life that I felt close to him.

Grandma having fun with Margaret & Emmie at family picnic, c. 1950

Zi Pasquale and his wife, Mauretta (Laura) or Zizi, as she was called by us, were not blessed with children; however, my grandmother and grandfather became the parents of six children—five girls and one boy—Mary, Elena (Helen, my mother), Emma, Lena, Virginia, and Raffela (Ralph, or Uncle Dick). My mother, as the second child, was the first of the six to be born in the United States in 1914, and she outlived all of her siblings. The four adults and the six children lived on the first floor of the house in five rooms with only two bedrooms—Grandma and Grandpa's room and the five girls in the other bedroom. Uncle Dick eventually slept in the living room on a day bed. They rented the second floor to another Italian family—the Passarellis.

Grandpa as a young man, c. 1908

LA FAMIGLIA

Grandpa and I in front of house on High Street, 1944

Marano girls, c. 1921. (My mom on the right.)

Zi Pasquale died of pneumonia well before I was born, so I never knew him, but I do know that he was an influential figure in my mother's life. From a lot of little details my mother shared with me over the years, I think that my mother inherited her *zio*'s strength of character and strong convictions.

I know little of what life was like when the two brothers and two sisters lived together in one household—only the few stories passed down. One story that is part of family lore is that Grandpa and Zi Pasquale were known to have a little too much to drink at times and they would FIGHT. I think that they were both very controlling men in their own way (very typical of Italian men!) and life may have been rather tumultuous at times in that

LA FAMIGLIA

Zi Pasquale and Zizi, c. 1930

house on High Street where the two couples and six children co-habitated. The men were in charge and the women were very deferential to their men, but Grandma and Zizi were both strong individuals in their own right and one might say that they really controlled things.

Grandpa was very influenced by and enamored with Gene Tunney, the heavyweight-boxing champion of the 1920s. When he learned that Gene Tunney quit drinking to enhance his health, Grandpa quit too. I don't remember Grandpa taking a drink—ever. I don't think he even drank the homemade wine that was on every Italian-American table. Grandpa was very interested in maintaining a healthy lifestyle, thus his daily walk, and no sweets (except for the four teaspoons of sugar in his espresso) and no alcohol became his regimen for the remainder of his life.

The two brothers were responsible for moving to America and establishing their family in America. They left a sister and other brothers behind. There had been nine siblings altogether, but the 1917 Influenza Epidemic took at least two of them. It was not an easy life in the south of Italy at the turn of the century, but that was the reason for taking the risk of leaving home. It was their fortitude and strength that gave their descendants the opportunities that followed. They showed such courage to travel so far and endure the hardship of an arduous trip, only to arrive in a new land facing an unknown future. I learned that nearly half of the Italian immigrants who came to America in the early 1900s eventually returned to Italy for one reason or another. It was the perseverance, endurance, and stamina of those who remained—including my grandparents—that created the Italian-American community. I am grateful to them for that.

Grandma and Zizi

Two sisters marrying two brothers—I'm not sure how unusual that was in those days. But the two sisters could not have been

LA FAMIGLIA

Grandma & Zizi as young girls, c. 1905

21

more different. My grandmother was a cuddly and warm human being, and as her first grandchild I especially felt her love. After giving birth to six children she was matronly in stature, and I think she wore a corset until the day she died. Despite the thick stockings she wore to control the edema in her legs and the heavy "old lady" shoes she wore daily, Grandma always looked nice and was well put together. She freshened herself up for dinner

Grandma and Grandpa in front room of house on High Street

every day sometimes pinning a Lily of the Valley from the garden to her dress. At the end of the day she presented herself as calm and composed even though she had spent the entire day cleaning and cooking. She had the most gorgeous fluffy white hair that was silky and slightly curly. It was her trademark. And she perpetually had a beautiful smile on her face.

While Grandpa was strict and stern, Grandma was the opposite for her children and her grandchildren. She was the one who tried to keep the peace at all times. I felt a comfortable sense of security around her. She had a great sense of humor and could laugh at almost anything. Although Grandma and Zizi would "go at it" with one another sometimes (I was definitely aware of arguments between them even as a young child) they could also laugh together, which was really fun to see.

And then there was Zizi. Zizi is the endearment term for *zia* or "aunt" in Italian. The sisters were different in attitude, sentiment and persona. Zizi was the typical little old Italian lady—covered from head to toe in black with her hair pulled back in the proverbial bun. She continued to wear black for the entire rest of her life (almost fifty years) after her husband, Pasquale, died. She was a character and she played an important role in all of our lives. She was an extremely strong-willed individual and favored a rather pessimistic outlook on life. Even though she could laugh heartily at times, she also worried a lot. I can still see her clasping her hands in front of her and saying "*Jesu! Marie!*" over and over again when she became upset about something.

Zizi was smaller in stature than Grandma. Although the older sister, she was shorter and more petite. Never having had children, her body didn't expand like other Italian women who gave birth to many children. My sister recently shared with me that my mother found a tiny baby bonnet stashed away in the bottom of a drawer in her upstairs room after Zizi passed away. Why was it there? What did that signify? Whether that meant that there had been a baby, a pregnancy or miscarriage, we'll never know.

Since Zi Pasquale and Zizi originally bought the house on High Street, Zizi became the sole owner when her husband died. Although the entire house belonged to her, she allowed her sister's family, with the six children, to live on the first floor, and she was content to call one room on the second floor hers. Zizi's room became a sort of secret place for my sister and me and for my cousins. On occasion one of us might be lucky enough—maybe we were misbehaving or just having a bad day—to be escorted up there after Sunday dinner and be invited into her private space. My sister even slept up there when Zizi babysat for her because in our day, only family took care of us. We NEVER had a baby sitter. As a matter of fact, one of my cousins asked to keep the screen door to Zizi's room when the house was ultimately sold. It held a special place in all of our hearts. Although the room upstairs was her retreat, Zizi was an integral part of the household downstairs. Frankly, the two dynamic sisters ruled the roost.

Without children of her own at home to care for—although she shared all of the household duties with Grandma—Zizi was also employed as a seamstress in a local dress factory. Her work and salary sometimes kept the larger family together. I remember accompanying her to the factory where she worked, as did so many Italian immigrant women, and while there I played with the gigantic spools of colorful thread.

LA FAMIGLIA

Grandma, Zizi, Aunt Mary and Mom c. 1915

Zizi and I somehow had a special bond since I was the eldest and only grandchild until I was four years old, and maybe because we were somewhat similar in nature. I shared a story with my husband about how she once said that I had a "terrible disposition" when, as a five-year old, I was beginning to exhibit my independent nature. Zizi was clear to inform my mother that she was rearing a much-too-strong-willed child. Ha. Alan brings that to my attention all the time—reminding me that he thinks Zizi was right as he looks up to the heavens and calls out "Zizi!" when I begin to show my adult strong-willed and aggressive behavior.

Zizi was also the one who kept up with most of the Italian traditions that were part of their early lives in Italy and brought from their homeland to America. She planted and tended the garden in the backyard to grow tomatoes and other vegetables that were the staples of Italian cuisine. While we lived at the house, it was my father who tended the garden and even after we moved to Yonkers, he helped Zizi plant and care for the garden for many years.

Zizi also maintained a root cellar in the basement of the house where she kept potatoes and onions and other root vegetables. Sometimes she took one of us kids down there to fetch something. It was very dark and you couldn't see much—none of us particularly cared to go down there. My sister has a vivid memory of a day when she was very young and she accompanied Zizi to the root cellar. After they got there Zizi started laughing uncontrollably. Emmie didn't know what Zizi had found so funny as she ran back upstairs rather frightened. It seemed that when Zizi bent down to pick up some potatoes, her false teeth fell out of her mouth and she was trying desperately in the dark to get them back into her mouth before my sister could see her without her teeth! That event became a family story that has been passed on by all—*when Zizi lost her teeth.*

Zizi carried her large black handbag wherever she went. And that pocketbook contained all of her important papers—it

LA FAMIGLIA

Zizi and Mom, c. 1933

was her traveling file cabinet. In it were her bankbook, mortgage papers, house deed, birth certificate, marriage certificate—the works. She was never without all of those vital documents.

We had fun with both Grandma and Zizi. We sat together upstairs on Sunday nights and watched *The Ed Sullivan Show* together. Grandpa placed his chair right in front of the television and the rest of us took our seats around him. The two women would both laugh and laugh, especially at the zany animal acts and Señor Wences. I can still see Grandma throwing her head back and laughing at something that tickled her. And Zizi was in the habit of talking back to the TV. Watching a show, she would invariably say things like, "*Watch out!*" "*He's right behind you!*" As kids we thought that was very funny. Her penchant for calling out was hilariously apparent when my sister played the lead role in her high school play *Junior Miss*. Zizi sat in the audience of the intimate Coal Bunker Theater at Gorton High School, Yonkers, New York, with the rest of the family who had come to see Emmie, the actress. Zizi continued to talk to her great-niece throughout the entire performance. At intermission Emmie's fellow cast members asked, "*Who is that little Italian woman!*" And Em answered, "*That's my Zizi!*" It is a very sweet memory for her.

Sometimes we teased Grandma and Zizi when their "broken English" made us giggle. Zizi might take us to the pantry to get a special treat—"chip potatoes" as she called them, or take the little ones to the china cabinet in the dining room before Sunday dinner, give them M&M's from the little green glass candy dish, and say, "*Don't tell Grandma.*"

LA FAMIGLIA

A favorite piece of memorabilia that I have is Zizi's antique spaghetti roller that she brought with her from Italy. It is made of brass and is about ten inches long with two handles, one on either end with ridges in the middle to roll over the semolina dough to make spaghetti strands. It has the initials "MD" on it—Mauretta DelZio. It is a prized possession of mine.

It was like having two Grandmas. They were very different from one another, but double the pleasure. We were very lucky.

Life at Home

I remember much about those years—as part of my extended Italian-American family when our little family lived downstairs. Zizi and Grandma cooked every day and we shared many meals with them—particularly Sunday dinner. Sundays at Grandma's were happy times for the entire family.

Sundays at Grandma's: Emma, Carl, Jean, and I, 1954

My mother and little sister and I had tea together every afternoon in our basement apartment. Grandma and Zizi came downstairs at four o'clock each weekday and as we drank our tea and enjoyed biscotti, we watched *The Kate Smith Hour* on our black-and-white 12-inch television. One afternoon while Zizi was pouring the hot water into the teapot to brew the tea, the lid came off and the boiling water fell onto my lap. I must have been five or six years old. Zizi was horrified by the accident. Quite a commotion followed. Grandma, Zizi and my mother hovered over me to make sure that I wasn't burned too badly. I was really okay, but the grownups were VERY upset—enough to make a serious impact on me.

The rest of the family—aunts, uncles, and cousins—came every Sunday for dinner.

Extended Marano family around the dining table, c. 1946

On most Sundays after all of the Maranos had married and grandchildren were born, there were seventeen people around

LA FAMIGLIA

Aunt Emma and I, 1944

the dining room table each and every week—at two o'clock. Around that table sat Aunt Mary and Uncle Bob with cousin Margaret, Aunt Ginny and Uncle Augie with cousins Carl and

Jean, Aunt Lena, Aunt Diane and Uncle Dick with cousins Richard and Joanne, Mom, Dad, Emmie and I, and Grandpa at the head of the table in his corner spot. Grandma and Zizi sat at the foot of the table—closest to the kitchen. Missing at the table was Aunt Emma, my mother's closest sister. Aunt Emma died when she was twenty-eight years old. I was a year old.

My sister was named after her. Aunt Emma had been married to Uncle Mike Locuratolo. After she passed and Uncle Mike married again, he remained loyal to Grandma and Grandpa and the entire Locuratolo family (lots of Locuratolos!) remained

Grandma in her kitchen

part of our extended family too. That's the way it was with large Italian families.

The menu was invariably the same for those Sunday dinners—fruit cocktail to start as an appetizer, then pasta or *primi piatti* (ziti, ravioli, or spaghetti), and then chicken or beef with vegetables as a main course or *secondi*. Salad came next which was followed by fruit and nuts to end the meal. For dessert Grandma made either an angel food cake, served with strawberries and whipped cream, or a pineapple upside-down cake, her specialty—all made from scratch. And all made with love.

We watched Grandpa at the end of the meal when Grandma placed his cup of espresso in front of him (served first—before anyone else). He poured four heaping teaspoons of sugar into his demitasse cup—stirred it once very swiftly, hardly touching the sugar granules, and then drank the dark liquid down leaving the sugar sediment in the bottom of the cup. It was a ritual. There was also a lot of chatter and laughter around the table. Everyone had fun. After the little kids left the table and went to play outside, I usually remained sitting at the table with the adults. I liked listening to the adult conversation. I remember some heavy political discussion between my mother and Uncle Augie that sometimes became very spirited.

Uncle Dick

Uncle Dick was single in the days when we lived in Mount Vernon and he was still part of the household upstairs. He was a young man in his thirties and was always entertaining to be around, especially for his nieces and nephew. We loved Uncle

Dick's car. It had a "rumble seat" in the back. It was such a thrill to be invited to sit in that rumble seat! Uncle Dick always seemed to make life more fun with some of his crazy antics.

Uncle Dick with his nieces and nephew

LA FAMIGLIA

Zizi with Emmie, Carl, and Margaret in front of their house

When I was two years old and Uncle Dick was still serving in the Army, he sent home a very special birthday gift for me. He had fashioned a Hawaiian grass skirt made out of parachute strings. He sent it to my mother with the most endearing handmade card (which I still have) explaining that he thought about me every

35

day and hoped I would like his little gift. That grass skirt was well worn. I played dress-up in it and spent many happy hours parading around in my grass skirt. My mother held on to it for many many years, but I fear that the thing kind of disintegrated eventually because of all the use it got. It was passed on to my little cousin Jean and she played with it as well.

Uncle Dick was a favorite guest during our family vacations with the Fusco family when we spent the month of July in Belmar, New Jersey. That time in Belmar is part of my most cherished childhood memories, but the height of the vacation for us was when Uncle Dick came to visit. The fun reached a peak with him around.

And, as kids, it was fascinating for us when Uncle Dick met Aunt Diane (eighteen years his junior) and they married. All of us—five grandchildren—were in attendance at that wedding, corsages, boutonnieres, and all. It was quite the occasion for us and for the entire family. There is a picture of Zizi and her great nieces and nephew in front of their house on the way to Uncle Dick's wedding looking prim and proper, but very proud. And for that momentous event, Zizi agreed to wear *navy blue* instead of her usual black!

And then there were the Sundays when the "Long Island Cousins" came to visit. Grandma and Zizi's cousin, Uncle Tom DelZio, lived in Jackson Heights, Queens, New York. On a whim Uncle Tom would pile his family—Aunt Mabel and Valerie and John—into their car and drive to Mount Vernon. Sometimes his other cousins, Raphaela and Arturo would join them. Their visit was always a surprise and one that we welcomed heartily. They invariably made the requisite stop at Arturo's, the Italian bakery at Hartley Circle in Mount Vernon before arriving at the house, bringing those delicious sfwilladel, macaroons, rum cakes, Italian cookies, and candy-coated almonds, Torrone and other Italian pastries. Boy, was that a treat. They entertained us with their stories and as youngsters we would giggle at Johnny's jokes and sense of humor. Valerie and John were several years older than my sister and I. At fourteen I was a junior bridesmaid in Valerie's wedding. They are still very much a part of our lives today and we still find Johnny as entertaining today as we did then. It was an event when they showed up in Mount Vernon and the discussion of how we were related became a never-ending conversation. Were we second cousins? Second cousins once removed? Twice removed? It went on forever.

A monumental celebration and milestone for the Marano family was Grandma and Grandpa's Fiftieth Wedding Anniversary. We certainly were not in the habit of celebrating anything lavishly, but for this occasion the entire family gathered together at the beautiful Tappan Hill Restaurant in Tarrytown, New York, for a special Sunday dinner. The location is magnificent overlooking the Hudson River and even then the interior was a sight to behold. Uncle Dick made the requisite toast to Grandma and Grandpa at the head table as we sipped our champagne. When he finished we heard a tinkling of glasses coming from the head table, as Grandma wanted everyone's attention. She said that she had something to say, too. She never failed to surprise. It wasn't Grandpa making that special toast—it was Grandma! She toasted her husband and his courage to leave Italy and come to America and then she turned to Zizi and recognized that Zizi would have been celebrating her fiftieth anniversary that year as well if Zi Pasquale had lived. She wanted everyone to recognize that fact. It was a very happy occasion for us. JoAnn Marano was a toddler at the time and the only member of the immediate family missing from this photo.

Marano family at Grandma and Grandpa's 50th Anniversary dinner

The Fuscos

I cannot leave this section on *La Famiglia* without explaining how much the Fusco family figured in our lives during my childhood and young adulthood. Our family and the Fusco family (we weren't blood relatives but we called them cousins) spent a lot of time together. The Fusco girls and Emmie and I were more like sisters growing up.

Auntie Edie was my mother's best friend. They knew each other from their high school days, although Auntie Edie was a few years old than Mom; Uncle Al knew my dad through my Uncle Harry Aurisy and his oil company. The two couples were fast friends while they were courting and then after their respective marriages. Both Auntie Edie and Uncle Al were Italian-American as well and their extended families became a part of our family too. Auntie Edie was Emmie's godmother and Mom and Dad were godparents to their daughter, Alberta.

Our little Patavino family of four did everything with the Fusco family of four. Every Friday night we got together at one another's home and watched *I Remember Mama* on TV and had coffee and cake before departing, using Mom or Auntie Edie's collection of china cups and saucers and cake plates. (I still have my mother's collection of different patterns.)

And we vacationed together —at the shore in Belmar, New Jersey. We rented a bungalow in Belmar for the month of July several years during our childhood. My mother and Auntie Edie and the four girls, Kathy, Bertie, Emmie and I spent the full month there each summer, and "the fathers" joined us on the weekends and for their one-week vacation from their jobs. Eight of us stayed in a little cottage and spent glorious days in the sun. We went to the beach every day and rode the beautiful waves endlessly. I remember getting into bed at night still feeling the rolling waves taking me onto shore. I loved it. We usually cooked out every night and Auntie Edie and Mom read to us from Louisa May Alcott's *Little Women* at bedtime. We got through the whole book during the month. Kathy, Annie, Bertie, and Emmie felt as if we were Meg, Jo, Beth, and Amy.

We also spent hours playing our favorite "game" or "playacting" as "Lucille and Danny." Lucille was my beautiful cousin on my father's side and at sixteen she met and fell in love with Danny Dondero and they got engaged and married. The grownups all felt they were "too young to fall in love" (like the Nat King Cole song "Too Young" implied), but we thought it was very romantic and we decided to role play their wedding

Kathy Fusco and me. c. 1945

over and over again. I played Lucille, Bertie played Danny, Kathy was the priest who married us, and Emmie was the little flower girl. Whenever boredom set in or we needed another activity we found ourselves saying, "Let's play Lucille and Danny again!"

We walked the boardwalk at the Jersey shore and would invariably get splinters in our feet. Uncle Al would line us up and remove those splinters for us. And we fondly remember the "Belmar cake"—a yellow cake with chocolate icing. Dad and Auntie Edie celebrated their birthdays during the month of July and the Belmar cake became a welcome ritual.

Auntie Edie and Mom were fashionable ladies and they were always turned out beautifully. They delighted in dressing their daughters fashionably too.

Mom made many of our dresses and she took us to the Little Empress coat factory in New York City each year to buy our winter coats and leggings wholesale. Although money was not plentiful, Mom and Auntie Edie did their best to give us a sense of style. We remember fondly our annual treks to New York City at Christmas time and Easter. Each year we saw the Christmas Show at Radio City Music Hall and visited St. Patrick's Cathedral and Rockefeller Center after which we ate lunch at Horn & Hardart's, the famous cafeteria-style restaurant where we put a quarter in the slot to get our sandwich-of-choice behind the glass window.

The extended Fusco family also figured in our lives. Our lives were so intertwined that Auntie Edie and Uncle Al's respective families became part of our extended family too. Uncle Al's mother was married twice, so there were Fusco offspring and Chase offspring. But on holidays everyone was together and we even called them "aunt" and "uncle" and "cousin." One of the younger cousins was David Chase. Bertie had a special relationship with David as they were close in age and did a lot together as children. Now you may recognize that name; David Chase is the creator, writer, and director of *The Sopranos*—the very famous and acclaimed HBO series. After college David moved to California and began his career as a screenwriter and TV writer. He was responsible for several successful series, like *I'll Fly Away, The Rockford Files,* and *Northern Exposure* . . . prior to the creation of *The Sopranos.*

David's father (Uncle Henry to me) had changed the family name to "Chase" from "DeCesare" long before David was born. Although he was born in Mount Vernon, he spent most of his childhood in the New Jersey suburbs of Clifton and North Caldwell. I cannot tell you how David knew so much about the "underworld" and the Mafia, but I do know that he was fascinated by it throughout his life. His Wikipedia biography states, "he grew up watching matinee crime films and was well known as a creative storyteller." That same bio also mentions that he "had many problems with his overbearing parents"; that his father was "an angry man who belittled him constantly"; and that his mother (Aunt Norma to me) was a "passive-aggressive drama queen and a nervous woman who dominated any situation she was in by being so needy and always on the verge of hysteria." David admitted early on that his *Sopranos* character, Livia (Tony Soprano's mother in the series), is based on his own mother. In fact, David spent a lot of time in the Fusco home during his childhood—perhaps a healthier environment than his own home, and Auntie Edie gave him the love and nurturing that he may have lacked at home. David spent the entire summer at the Fusco house for many years during his childhood.

I remember sitting in my kitchen in Boston after *The Sopranos* had premiered on HBO, reading an article in the *New York Times* about the popular new show—and it was all about David Chase. I jumped up and said, "That's little David!!!!" After the show enjoyed several successful seasons, I read that David was to be interviewed on *60 Minutes*. Prior to that my sister had sent a picture to David in California that we found in our family

Extended Fusco family with our family, Christmas, 1955 (David Chase in foreground being chastised by his mother.)

album that included David and his mother and father, together with our family and several other members of the Fusco and Chase families. When the *60 Minutes* show aired I was sitting at home watching the telecast listening to David's interview when the photo that Emma sent him appeared on the screen. There I was bigger than life! What a shocker.

David invited his cousins Bertie and Kathy to Radio City Music Hall for every new season premier of *The Sopranos*. He may not have had the joyous childhood that we all remembered, but he understands the importance of one's roots. Throughout the series there is evidence of that fact in that David chose to use many names from his youth and childhood in telling the story. It is a great feeling to know that he was part of our extended family as we were growing up and we are so proud of all of his marvelous accomplishments.

Essentially, there were three Italian families that contributed to my beautiful childhood memories—the Maranos, the Patavinos, and the Fuscos. All of these people enriched the loving environment that I was so fortunate to be a part of. As the toast at the closing of the film *Moonstruck* emphasizes *"LA FAMIGLIA!!!"*

Buon Natale
et Buona Pasqua

In an Italian-American household holidays are always elaborate and special. I can still remember Grandma and Zizi rolling the pasta dough as we walked into the house and then seeing the homemade ravioli laid out on Grandma and Grandpa's bed waiting to be dumped into the boiling water. In an Italian household every holiday meal started with pasta whether it was Christmas dinner or Easter dinner, and, yes, even the American holiday of Thanksgiving. By the way, we called it "*gravy*" not "*sauce*," and "*macaroni*" not "*pasta*." In those days we knew little else other than spaghetti or ziti or ravioli.

And who could forget the special holiday baking—zeppellis and struffola at Christmas; tarrelle, pizza rustica (meat pie), and ricotta pie at Easter.

Christmas Eve

Christmas Eve dinner, The Feast of the Seven Fishes, consisted of pasta alla olia, eel and baccala (cod fish) and other fishes, eggplant, and salad. The tastes, textures, and smells remain with me to this day. I have tried my best to carry on those traditions by making some or all of those special dishes from the recipes handed down to me by my mother (not from Grandma, because, like every other real Italian cook, she never used a recipe!) for our holiday celebrations today. I'm happy that my daughter, Leigh, has made some of these dishes too, so that they will pass on after my sister and I are gone.

Christmas Eve dinner was the most memorable of all the holiday get-togethers for the family. Christmas Eve dinner was meatless like every Friday in a Catholic household. There were supposed to be twelve different dishes (mostly fish), which represented Christ and the twelve disciples at the table. There are many variations on the origin of the fish story, but we stuck with our rendition and always counted the number of separate items on the table. There were probably more than twelve if you counted the nuts and the fruit and the wine. Not only was the meal so traditional and extravagant, the whole evening was fun especially for the kids. After dinner was cleared away and dishes were done and the dining room table remained with just the table pads on it, the cards came out. My cousins and I collected as many pennies as possible from the adults to play *Twenty-One*. EVERYONE played—from the oldest to the youngest—contributing to our sense of family. We played other games too, like *Pass the Scissors* and *Coffee Pot*.

We loved it. And then—we opened presents! When we were young we exchanged gifts with our cousins and there were packages for all of us from Grandma and Grandpa and from Zizi. Because there weren't any gifts for the adults Grandma created a grab bag, with ribbons and all, so that the adults had something to open. She always outdid herself. Each year her gag gifts became funnier and more creative. It was a happy time and we were a happy family. We laughed a lot and there were the typical jokes and making fun of family members. Inevitably, Uncle Augie would entertain us with his imitation of the various and outlandish types of sneezes and nose blowing within the family, which most assuredly drew an audience and a laugh.

The Christmas tree stood in the sunroom at the front of the house. It wasn't very large, but it was a beautiful sight for us to behold. The live evergreen tree was decorated with old-fashioned candle-like bulbs that had bubbles in them that moved up and down. Those lights replaced the original ones that were made of real wax candles. One year when my sister, Emma, and two of my little cousins, Carl and Margaret, were toddlers, the entire tree fell over on them causing much commotion within the household. Presumably the three little tykes were playing under the tree and—boom—down it came! It was a mess to clean up, but the little ones were okay—not so with some of the Christmas balls and lights.

Easter

At Easter, beside the Easter breads and pies, dinner started with ravioli or manicotti, and lamb or rabbit was also on the menu. In addition to all of that Grandma created a basket made of dough with a braided handle and a colored hard-boiled egg inside of it. There was one for each of her grandchildren. Grandma also managed to organize an Easter egg hunt with plastic colorful eggs and filled them with pennies and hid them both inside and outside. All the kids loved the hunt.

And Easter breakfast was spent with the Fuscos. After attending Easter Mass we gathered at one of our houses—Mom and Auntie Edie and we four girls in our Easter finery sporting

Mom, Dad, Emma and I, Easter, 1950

Mom, Dad, Emma and I, Easter, 1960

corsages from Dad and Uncle Al—and we shared a delicious breakfast of the traditional Easter baked goods our moms had prepared. We were all decked out in our new Easter outfits—a really big deal for us. Each year Dad went to Yedowitz florist on the day before Easter to get our corsages—an orchid for Mom, a gardenia for me, and pink roses for Emmie.

And ten years later—still the same Easter-morning ritual.

It is no wonder that holiday celebrations stick in my mind so vividly.

Quatiere

I also distinctly recall the cultural atmosphere of a predominantly Italian-American enclave in the neighborhood—on High Street in Mount Vernon. Most houses had a grape arbor in the backyard and some houses even had a bocce court (an Italian game played with balls similar to lawn bowling) too. I remember sitting under the arbor on hot Sunday afternoons in the summer. We knew all of the neighbors and everyone was very friendly and neighborly, although we never shared meals together or entered one another's homes. Aurelio lived next door and we could hear him playing his mandolin under his grape arbor on warm summer nights.

The grape arbor was such an Italian thing. When the grapes were ripe in late summer/early fall, we could reach up and grab a bunch. They were sweet and tasty. In the fall my mother and Grandma and Zizi made grape jam from both the green and the dark red Concord grapes. The dark red grapes were the ones used for the wine that Zizi made—the wine that accompanied every meal—with little tastes even for the children. The young ones were offered a tablespoon of wine with water added in a pretty pony glass. It was a first taste of wine in front of the whole family.

Our entire gang gathered under the arbor for the "mortgage burning party" in 1964 after Zizi made the final payment on the house. It became a major family event and a celebration of historic significance. Everyone was present—aunts, uncles, cousins, neighbors.

We also "stoop sat" each night on the brick steps leading up to the front door—the whole crew outside—cheerily greeting neighbors as they walked by during their *passeggiata*, the Italian custom of an evening walk. Wooden chairs were brought outside from indoors—no lawn chairs. This is such a typical sight in any Italian neighborhood or household whether in Italy or America.

My younger cousin, Jean Sousa, recalls one of those evenings with a story she loved. I'm not sure whether she was there to witness it, but she certainly remembered the story as told when, *Annie had ants in her pants!* It seems that I sat on some ice cream that had fallen on the stairs where ants had collected to scoop the ice cream up and I sat down on it—ice cream, ants, and all. And the ants got into my pants! Zizi in her frantic haste dragged me into the house to dump me in the bathtub, exclaiming once again, *"Jesu Marie! Jesu Marie!"* As a little girl, Jean thought that was the most hilarious story she had ever heard.

I also recall the fruit truck that appeared on the street—sometimes twice a week—selling fresh produce right at your doorstep. In those days the milkman, the iceman, the fruitman, and other men in trucks were common sights in the neighborhood streets. I'm sure it is the way it was in the old country and these folks who had traveled so far across the sea kept the old rituals alive as much as possible. That memory came back to me years later when my daughter and I visited my paternal grandparents' village in Montelongo, Italy, and I was awakened by the clear shouts of "*Frutta! Frutta!*" in the streets below their home.

To replenish the pantry with other groceries and cooking staples, Grandma needed only to pick up the heavy black telephone that sat on a small stand between the dining room and living room and place her order with the neighborhood grocery store—Marcianti's. And the order was then delivered within an hour or two. When we lived in the basement apartment I was old enough to be entrusted with the small change it took to buy milk or something else my mother may have needed, walk to Marcianti's and make the requisite purchase. Everyone shopped at Marcianti's. The small neighborhood store supplied all of the good food to the Italian homes for many years—olive oil, cheeses, salami, mortadella, cappicola, breads, and on and on. On one of my errands to the store little sister Emma and cousin Carl tagged along with me and we bought a loaf of Italian bread. By the time we got home the loaf was almost gone! Those rascals kept taking bites along the way. I'm sure I had some too.

As a youngster I tagged along with Zizi as she volunteered at St. Anthony's Feast (*la festa*—Italian bazaar or street fair) which took place each summer not too far from the house. Zizi worked a booth during the afternoons selling the Italian candies—nougat and bars with almonds—and I sat there continually tasting bits of the yummy stuff. Zizi also brought me along with her when she visited Our Lady of Mount Carmel Church on Holy Thursday at Easter time to bring a basket of bread and food to leave on the altar.

Religion

Zizi was the only one in the family who remained Catholic after arriving in America, although she didn't go to Mass regularly. As the story goes, my grandfather was not that pleased with the Catholic Church after his arrival in America because he felt the church was unwelcoming to the Italian immigrants like himself and his family. I am not sure what Zi Pasquale's religious preferences were and whether the two brothers were at odds on that issue; however, after Zi Pasquale passed away Grandpa was head of the household and the rest of the family followed him. Respect for authority—mainly for parents and elders—is a foundation of Italian life, but there was also suspicion of other authority figures such as politicians and the Catholic hierarchy. Whether that was what drove my grandfather away from the Catholic Church toward the Episcopal Church is unknown, but not unlikely.

A friend of the family began attending the nearby Episcopal Church and Grandpa soon followed along. Eventually he became good friends with the Episcopal parish priest and joined his congregation. All of the Marano children of my mother's generation were raised in that church, and I presume they attended regularly until they were adults and married. I never remember Grandma going to church, however. She probably had her own opinions on the matter, but Grandma never opposed Grandpa because he was the ruler of his domain. Instead she quietly kept her religious beliefs to herself. She did her own thing and was most likely excused from church services because she needed to cook or care for the younger ones. But Zizi remained Catholic throughout her lifetime, carried the rosary beads wherever she went, and upheld the Catholic doctrine. My sister tells me that she still has some bits and pieces of Zizi's rosary beads in her jewelry box and has saved them as a treasured keepsake.

This religious difference distinguished my mother's family from other Italian-American families. All of my aunts and uncle (including my mother) converted back to Catholicism when they married, because they invariably fell in love with Italian Catholics and it was just expected that their household would be a Catholic one and that their children would be raised Catholic. In fact, both my mother and Uncle Dick received their confirmation at Christ the King Church in Yonkers, New York, when my sister and I received that sacrament in 1956.

I learned later that this was not as unusual as I thought. Other Italian immigrants did not feel especially welcomed by the Catholic Church after their arrival in America—just as my grandfather perceived. Because the Irish immigrants preceded the Italians, they became the ones in charge—in politics, in the church, and within other institutions. Even after she converted to Catholicism my mother said that she missed the choir singing at the Episcopal Church and she never could understand "confession," but she lived out her life as a practicing Catholic for my father's sake and for that of her children.

Music

I assume that music played a role in my grandparents' household too, but I have no memory of listening to opera or other Italian music. What I do remember is the large upright piano with its spool-legged stool that sat in the living room. On the Sundays that we were all there for dinner we kids would take turns rolling the stool around the living room and twirling ourselves around and around on the stool. What fun that was. I honestly have no recall of any of the adults sitting at the piano and playing, other than my mother when she helped me practice after my lessons. While we lived at the house I was lucky enough to have piano lessons with Professor Console.

Professor Console was a friend of Grandpa's who was the consummate Italian renaissance figure with his mustache and long hair. I do not know how and why he and Grandpa became friends, but he also taught my mother the violin when she was a girl.

My mother apparently was the only one of her siblings who had any musical talent or aspirations. She must have had piano lessons, too, because she knew how to read music and was able to make sure that I practiced after my lessons. Professor Console visited the Marano home regularly to just pop in to say *buon giorno* to Grandpa and he came once a week to give me my piano lesson. Perhaps Grandpa made him new eyeglasses and in return I got piano lessons! As I got a little older I walked to his studio on Fourth Avenue in Mount Vernon for my weekly lesson. That was an experience too. When I was seven or eight years old Professor Console's studio was sort of a scary place. Other students were there as I walked in—voice, violin, cello students—and I felt rather intimidated. His was a formidable presence. I must have done fairly well because I continued with piano lessons once we moved to Yonkers. I only wish I had stuck with it longer.

QUATIERE

Helen Marano with her violin, c. 1927

I'd also like to think that some of the influence of Professor Console and the Marano household had the tiniest effect on my musician son, David, and that his musical talent was inherited from that side of the family. David is a percussionist—classical, jazz, pop, rock—and has had a very active career in both New York City and Las Vegas, Nevada, where he now lives.

Transitions

All of this was my frame of reference as I was growing up. Even after we moved to Yonkers, we still went to Grandma's for Sunday dinner and occasionally Grandma, Grandpa, Zizi, and Aunt Lena came to our house. Dad drove to Mount Vernon to pick them up and then drove them back home in the evening. Grandpa never learned how to drive nor did they ever have a family car. Our Yonkers house, with my father's beautifully tended backyard, became the center of many family gatherings as the years moved on. First communions, graduations, christenings, and confirmations were all celebrated there.

There was a distinct cultural shift, however, when we moved to Yonkers. My mother was a very bright and strong-willed woman who always knew what she wanted. And she wanted her little family out of Mount Vernon! Mom never got the opportunity to go to college. She excelled at school, graduated summa cum laude from Mount Vernon High School (she scored 100% on her history Regents exam), and trained as an executive secretary. She worked in New York City as a secretary before she was married. She constantly envisioned herself moving up in the world and she worked hard to make that happen. Shortly after we moved to Yonkers, she began working again as a secretary. I was probably the only one in my class who had a working mother. She was ahead of her time and she made things happen for our little family.

Backyard at Morsemere Ave.

The cultural shift was symbolized from stoop sitting in the front on High Street to enjoying our beautiful backyard lawn and lovely garden on summer evenings in Yonkers. It was a distinct difference.

This was my life well into my college years. Zizi passed away after suffering a stroke. Grandma was in the hospital when Zizi died and was not able to attend her sister's funeral. I remember feeling rather stunned about that; the two sisters who were so close during their entire lifetime, and Grandma couldn't be there to say goodbye. Grandma passed away when I was in my first year of teaching in 1966. My sister was away at school at the time and I was the only grandchild at hand. I remember being at the hospital before Grandma went into surgery for a hiatal hernia. As she was being rolled away on the gurney, she waved her hand to us standing behind—to me, my mother and father and Uncle Dick. That was the last we saw her. She died on the operating table. She was seventy-three years old.

My memories of my dad and Uncle Dick returning to the house after she passed are vivid to this day. My mother and I went back home to sit and wait with Grandpa, and Dad and Uncle Dick had remained at the hospital awaiting word following her surgery. We sat in the sunroom watching intently for their return. When they walked into the house and informed us all, "She's gone," turmoil ensued. Aunt Diane ran upstairs to the apartment where she and Uncle Dick then lived. She had become very close to Grandma having lived in the same house for so long and she felt her loss tremendously. Aunt Ginny, who suffered from depression for a good portion of her adult life, needed a doctor's attention and a shot to calm her. I remember my cousin Carl needing to carry his mother into a bedroom so that Dr. Loebs could attend her. All the while, Grandpa sat with his head in his hands just shaking his head back and forth. I also remember sitting in the kitchen with my mother as we got ready to depart for the night, and I asked her, "*Why aren't you crying?*" Her answer to me was, "S*omeone has to be strong.*"

Emma flew home for the funeral and I was delegated the task to fetch her at the airport. Losing Grandma was monumental to all of us. Emma remembers that we all went shopping together to buy black outfits. It was expected. I remember still wearing my black outfit when I returned to my teaching job in Briarcliff Manor, New York, as I attended a faculty meeting after the funeral. I think my very Anglo colleagues couldn't understand that the death of your Italian grandmother was an enormous loss.

Grandma's passing was an event in my life that showed me the immense strength that both my mother and my father exhibited in moments of stress, crisis and sadness. I continued to observe that throughout my life. Dad might get emotional reading a greeting card and we would find ourselves smiling affectionately as his voice cracked, but he was a true rock when it counted and he could pull it together at the big moments, time and time again.

With both Grandma and Zizi gone, it was definitely the end of an era. There were even some difficult family divides that occurred in the years that followed (mainly over the High Street house), but luckily they healed after several years of unrest. Grandpa lived to be eighty-one; his final years were spent in a nursing home. He was never really the same after losing his wife.

Paternal Grandparents

Formal portrait of Patavino family, c. 1918

And what about my father's Italian family? It is ironic that although it was my mother's family that was so influential in my childhood, it was my father's family that I have researched more fully and it is that line that enabled my daughter and me to achieve our dual citizenship. We were able to find living relatives and even visit the family home where my grandmother Patavino was born in Montelongo, Italy, in the Molise region. All of that was incredible, and thanks to my daughter

Michele Patavino and brother (?), 1903

PATERNAL GRANDPARENTS

Leigh, my father was able to learn more about his family and his heritage before he died. He knew little up to that point about his family's background with just bits of information relayed from his older brother and sister.

My father's father, Michele Patavino, died before Dad was born, so he never knew him. In fact, as the story goes, Grandpa Patavino had his bags packed and ready to go back to Italy because of his displeasure with life in America. He would have been part of that fifty per cent of Italians who returned to their homeland, never to be naturalized in the U.S.

Dad at 6 months old with Aunt Lucy, 1911

However, tuberculosis intervened and he was too sick to travel, and he subsequently died, leaving my grandmother with four children, which included a newborn baby—my father.

She was very poor and took in washing to make ends meet. The Jewish doctor who delivered my father knew of Grandma Patavino's dilemma and he kindly and graciously offered to take the baby and adopt him.

But my grandmother would have none of that. She struggled mightily, but she kept her family together with the help of her older sons, my Uncle Patty and Uncle John. Dad died of kidney failure two days after his ninety-second birthday. His renal doctor, Dr. Germain, was at his side along with my mother and my sister and me as he passed away. One of his last statements to us was *"A Jewish doctor brought me into this world, and a Jewish doctor will take me out."*

When my father was very young he and his two older brothers and sister lived in the Wakefield section of the Bronx, New York. His brothers were fourteen and fifteen years older than Dad and his sister, my Aunt Lucy. The older boys had to provide for their widowed mother and siblings, and my father was forced to leave school after the seventh grade to go to work to carry his own weight. Although that was the extent of his education, Dad was very skilled at building things and he was good at mathematics.

He was also a very good athlete. He excelled at tennis and was a champion bowler. He taught me to play tennis and I loved playing with him—even into his late eighties! He always said that he wished he could have been a surgeon. He was fascinated with the human body and how it worked and how science could

Dad at his first communion

improve conditions. Dad was extremely meticulous and cared for his home and garden with the utmost care. His car was always his pride and joy. He knew everything there was to know about automobiles, and he worked in his brother's automotive business

Dad holding cat

PATERNAL GRANDPARENTS

for most of his adult life. I believe that my son David is channeling him every time I learn about David's projects in his Las Vegas home or with his car—a 1965 Buick Riviera. I just know that Dad is standing right next to him saying, "Good job, David."

It wasn't until Aunt Lucy married Uncle Harry that Grandma Patavino moved from the Bronx into a larger home at

Grandma Patavino and I, 1944

180 Brookside Avenue in Mount Vernon, New York. I remember holiday meals at that house as well. Sadly, Uncle John, Dad's middle brother, died before I was born, so I never knew him. My cousins on that side—Eileen and Claire, Uncle Patty and Aunt Eileen's daughters, and Harriet, Lucille, and Eddie, Aunt Lucy and Uncle Harry's children—were six to twelve years older than me, so there wasn't the same kind of interaction with them as with my younger cousins on my mother's side. I grew up not having any cousins of my own age. That is why the Fusco girls, Kathy and Bertie, were so important to me.

My father's mother, Maria Micone, died when I was five years old. I remember her only slightly. I have some recall of when she was ill before she died and needed to be carried downstairs for a Thanksgiving dinner at Aunt Lucy's house. That part of my life is memorable through pictures more than anything else. There are pictures of me when I was two years old—my dad in his Army uniform and me with his hat on my head—in front of the house on Brookside Avenue with Grandma Patavino.

To me she seemed to be a soft and gentle lady, but my sister informed me that my mother told her that Grandma Patavino was a "castrating female!" Hmmmmmm. Didn't know that, and I don't know how much her life and difficulties impacted my father's life. My father was a generous and kind human being, liked and loved by everyone who knew him. I guess my mother had a different opinion of her mother-in-law! Whatever her personality, Maria Micone did have a hard life and my father's childhood was certainly not the same loving atmosphere that my mother knew. But the combination of my parents' childhood experiences made for a very wonderful life for my sister and me, and we are forever grateful for that.

Mom, Dad, and I, 1944

These are just some of the memories that have stayed with me. They are fond memories of a bygone era—of the struggles, the joys, and the ups and downs of my relatives as they made their way from one culture to another—from one country to another. I feel proud to be Italian-American and I really love being able to reminisce about the way life was then.

Growing Up Italian-American

So what was it like growing up as an Italian-American in the '40s, '50s, and '60s?

After the war was over, America became the melting pot, helped along by American soldiers bringing home war brides and Europeans seeking a fresh new start after leaving behind their ravaged homelands; immigrant cultures entered the mainstream. The Second World War also proved to be part of Italian-American assimilation into American culture as many Italian-Americans were soldiers serving in the American military.

As a result a greater understanding of different cultures emerged, but there was still discrimination. And Italian-Americans most assuredly felt that.

We were teased about being Italian-American. Derogatory terms like *Dago*, *Wop*, and *Guinea* were prevalent and even some of my best friends in high school would use those labels. I never paid much attention to it, but it did make me feel uneasy at times, although we knew it was just good-natured humor.

Many Italians encountered prejudice and negative stereotypes and were often victimized by the reputation of organized crime.

Notwithstanding some of the negative labels, all of America loved Italian-American singers like Frank Sinatra, Dean Martin, Perry Como, Vic Damone, Jerry Vale, and Tony Bennett. But Italian-Americans had a special affinity because they were theirs. My dad especially loved listening to his record collection, which consisted mainly of those singers as well as Tony Mattola, the guitarist, and Montovani orchestra recordings.

We delighted in the weekly TV shows that Frank Sinatra, Perry Como, and Dean Martin hosted. By the time those shows aired on TV, the Italian-American community had become more mainstream and accepted and every ethnicity enjoyed Frank and Perry and Dean's easy and smooth mannerisms and velvety voices—and the fun that they seemed to always have. One regret in life of mine is that I never saw *The Rat Pack* in Las Vegas—the live show that included Frank Sinatra, Dean Martin, Sammy Davis, Jr., Joey Bishop, and Peter Lawford. It would have been possible for me to do that, but I never took the initiative to make it happen.

It seemed everyone enjoyed pizza too. It is the gift to America from Italy. Pizza was a date-night essential during the '50s and '60s, and everyone had their favorite spots. And being from New York, we all knew there was nothing like New York pizza! But one needs to travel to Italy and eat pizza in Naples to truly understand what good pizza tastes like—*buono, buono*.

Thursday night was macaroni night at our house. The gravy sat on the stove simmering all day. Mom sautéed meatballs (with raisins because that's the way Dad liked them), sausage (both sweet and hot), spare ribs, and brasciole and added all of it to the gravy. She even used chicken feet for added flavor. Believe it or not, I liked them and I'd sneak a few out of the pot before we sat down to our dinner and devour them in a slurping sort of way. Dipping a slice from a fresh loaf of Italian bread into the simmering sauce was a no-no, but a divine experience if you could get away with it.

During my freshman year at SUNY Cortland I became close friends with Joanne Puglisi from Binghamton, New York. Joanne was a junior transfer student who lived in my dorm and she pledged my sorority with me. With only two years together on campus, our friendship went beyond being school friends as she asked me to accompany her home to Binghamton on weekends from time to time. Hers was a very different Italian family from mine. Joanne was considerably younger than her brothers—ten to fifteen years younger—and her parents were older (almost as old as my grandparents). Her mother stayed home each day in her housedress and cooked and cleaned just like my Grandma did. *My* mother went to work each day and wore stockings and heels. Joanne's father sat in his basement kitchen dressed in his white undershirt and made wine and gravy—just like the Italian men in the movies. *My* father went to work each day and was proud of the life he had carved out for himself and his family.

I loved the time I spent with Joanne and her family. It gave me a glimpse of another world. Her home was very close to the site of the infamous Mafia gathering of the '50s—the Apalachin Meeting. Not to suggest that there was any connection to the Puglisi family, but it brought to light how different my experiences as an Italian-American were from those of other Italian-Americans.

It was common practice to think that every Italian-American was Mafia connected. At least that's what other ethnicities thought. The media played into that. But it was not until the '70s and '80s, when films like *The Godfather I and II*, *Casino*, and *Goodfellas* hit the big screen that a closer view was available to all. Actors like Brando, DeNiro, and Pacino became so popular in America. It gave everyone a glimpse into that world; exposing us to both sides of Italian culture—the good and the bad.

I'd like to think that the discrimination Italian-Americans were subjected to in the first half of the twentieth century finally disappeared in the second half when other Italian-Americans became recognized leaders and contributors to our American life—Joe DiMaggio, Fiorello LaGuardia, Mario Lanza, Enrico Fermi, Francis Ford Coppola, Frank Stella, Mario Cuomo, as well as the singers and actors mentioned earlier. Theirs is a huge contribution to American culture.

PART TWO

Travels in Italy

Overview

I have traveled to Italy several times in my adult life. Each trip was better than the last and each trip has been memorable in its own way. My first trip was in 1967 when I was teaching school in Briarcliff Manor, New York. My college roommate, Ann Hull Thacher, and I decided that our summer would be spent traveling through Europe, and Italy was most certainly on the list of countries to visit. We spent a total of four days in Italy, and they were some of the best days of the entire trip.

My next voyages to the country of my ancestors were with family members, i.e. my daughter and my first husband Keith. Those sojourns helped to solidify my appreciation of my Italian roots and to see and learn more about the country.

In 2002 my daughter and I got to spend the most glorious and incredible four days in Montelongo, Italy, the town where my paternal grandmother was born. It was there that we learned so much about our relatives and our heritage.

That experience was followed by our two trips in 2010 and 2012 with my husband, Alan. We were married in March of

2010 and the trip to Italy was to be our honeymoon later that year in November when we could get away. Leigh accompanied us in 2010 as she embarked on a new life and new job in Italy. It was also the start of our journey to become Italian citizens. And by 2012 Leigh was living in Ostuni (*La Cita Bianca*) in the region of Puglia. We stayed with her in the apartment she was renting for the duration of that trip. (An interesting aside is that Leigh was contacted by *House Hunters International,* and she was featured in a segment for their HGTV show.)

Those two trips most assuredly made the desire to spend extended periods of time in the south of Italy all the more enticing to us. We even started looking at property and thought that we might buy a Trullo (the type of structure so common in Puglia) and possibly begin a renovation project.

On every single one of my trips, my cousin Piera Fogliato (whom I met in 1967 when she was twelve years old) nurtured our relationship with her family by meeting up with us at some point. She became such an integral part of our Italian experiences. In the years between my first two trips to Italy, my parents traveled there twice and connected with Piera's family in Torino. Piera's mother was my mother's first cousin. In 1985 Piera came to America to visit her cousins stateside. She even got to visit my immediate family on Martha's Vineyard during that trip. My sister and brother-in-law made a trip to Italy in the late '90s, and their sons also visited Piera in Torino. In fact, my nephews had been traveling in Europe at the time of 9/11 in the U.S. They felt they needed the comfort of home at that most difficult time and went "back home" to Piera in Torino to be with family. My daughter, on her many trips to Italy, always connected with Piera. Piera became our "Italian Connection." She has hosted so many of our family in her lovely apartment many times over, and she has made each of those experiences much more indelible. Piera attended both of my nephews' weddings—the first one in Edinburgh, Scotland, and the second in New Orleans, Lousiana. There is no question that she is a member of our inner family.

First Trip – 1967

My very first trip to Italy was part of a two-month European tour in the summer of 1967 with my college roommate Ann. We spent many months planning the trip. It was an awesome trip for both of us, but especially for me and for my family, as none of my relatives had ever traveled to Europe before. More importantly, I would get to visit my grandfather's sister and her family in Turin (*Torino*) once we got to the north of Italy.

We meticulously planned our itinerary, making some reservations at pensions and small hotels, but we also left several days open for flexibility and spontaneity. It was the year that the film "*If It's Tuesday . . . It Must Be Belgium*" was released, a film which exactly depicted our experience. We visited nine countries in seven weeks—Holland, Germany, Switzerland, France, Belgium, Denmark, Norway, Great Britain, and, of course, Italy. I diligently kept a log of the entire trip making entries every night before going off to sleep. And I took pictures. Boy, did I take pictures—hundreds of slides. Some of them were actually pretty good. Two carousels of slides were developed after we returned home and for some reason those carousels remained in my parents' possession. My sister was still at home at the time and she clearly remembers how proud Mom and Dad were about my trip; they showed the slides to everyone who came to visit them. Emmie would say, "Oh, no, not the slides again!" Even though she was subjected to watching them over and over again, she thought some of them were pretty good, too.

In 1967 I was twenty-four years old and had just completed my second year of teaching junior high school English in Briarcliff Manor, New York. Ann was an elementary teacher in Huntington, New York. We'd talked about making this trip for a long time. The following year we rented an apartment together in New York City. To this day we can still reminisce about our crazy experiences and the wild, wonderful, wacky, and fun time we had. It was a trip filled with laughs and fun experiences—every single day. The following Christmas, Ann presented me with the most spectacular gift—a scrapbook of our adventure. It was filled with mementos, pictures, and poems penned by Ann about our exploits—a genuine treasure.

We left Kennedy airport in New York and arrived at Schiphol Airport in Amsterdam, The Netherlands. Our round-trip airfare was $239. We had our trusty copy of *Europe on $5 a Day* clutched in our hands for the entire trip. It was our bible for the two months we were in Europe. We budgeted no more than $500 each for everything—hotels, food, transportation, gifts, etc. Somehow we did it on that!

Prior to the trip I was in the market to buy a new car and after researching the prospect, I ordered a brand-new red Karmann

FIRST TRIP—1967

Ann and I at the Colisseum, Rome, Italy

Ghia convertible—a very cool and sophisticated automobile! We arranged to pick up the car in Frankfurt, Germany. It was our means of transportation for a good portion of the trip. Having the car made our journey even more fun and exciting—and adventurous—as well as economical.

Before leaving the States for the trip I needed a few lessons on how to drive a stick-shift car. My brother-in-law, Ed Migdal, took me to a parking lot and we made a few turns around, which was significantly less preparation than necessary. Once Ann and

I arrived in Frankfort and picked up the car at the dealership, it became so obvious that my driving skills were lacking. In the middle of the hustling and bustling city of Frankfurt, Germany, I found myself stuck in the middle of trolley tracks and I could not put my new little Karmann Ghia into reverse to get us off the tracks. The driver descended from his seat on the trolley, pushed me out of the driver's seat of my car, and moved the car off the tracks before returning to his trolley. All the while, the passengers and the people in the surrounding area looked on and laughed their heads off. It was a great story that has been retold many times over.

Climbing The Simplon Pass (a rather formidable drive to say the least) from Italy into Switzerland in the rain was also a hair-raising experience. I was still learning how to control my new little car as Ann sat beside me with her heart in her mouth most of the time.

The car cost $2100, all paid for before we left on our trip, and an additional $200 to ship it back to the states from Le Havre, France. Having the car and driving through the countryside added so much to the trip. Ann called it "Little Ghia." It sure was fun riding with the top down all over Europe. I wish I still had it today.

After we shipped the car home (my father picked up my beautiful little car in New York), we continued to enjoy the final weeks of our trip. We traveled through Scandinavia and then spent a few days in London, after which we returned to Amsterdam where our adventure had begun. Then it was back to the States for the start of the new school year.

We had so much fun each and every day on our trip. We met fantastic people in every city we visited and even ran into some of our college friends along the way. It never ceased to amaze us that no matter where we were in the world, we might meet up with Cortland friends and even Sig Rho sisters—totally unplanned and unscripted.

My Karmann Ghia and I

From Amsterdam we took a train to Cologne, Germany, and then a trip down the Rhine River before picking up the car in Frankfurt. We then continued driving through Germany and into Italy where we made stops in Florence, Venice and Rome. Rome became a highlight for me because I decided to cut my very long dark-brown hair and have it frosted. Yikes, what a change. Ann and I visited a hair salon our first day in Rome and I tried to explain what I wanted to do. Whomever we met with that day spoke English and they understood—so we thought! When we returned the next day for our appointments, nobody spoke English. Although I experienced some severe anxiety over what I was doing, it all turned out just fine. I walked in with long dark hair and when I walked out I was a blonde! But I was happy and everyone seemed to like the drastic change. It most certainly made for dramatic memories of Rome.

During our days in Italy we constantly heard a pop tune on the radio and we began singing it loudly as we drove through the countryside and into the cities. The song was *Stasera Mi*

Lunch by the roadside after I became a blonde!

Butto by Rocky Roberts, a black singer originally from Alabama who became popular in Italy with the release of his recording in 1967. We even purchased cassette tapes of the song to bring back to the States. In today's technological era I was able to find You-Tube videos of Rocky Roberts singing his famous Italian song—along with his very cool moves. He was still making those videos well into the '80s.

Torino

Nothing about our fabulous trip could compare, though, with the two days we spent with my relatives in Torino, Italy. My grandfather wrote to his sister's family to tell them that I would be arriving sometime that summer. My grandfather had not seen his sister in more than fifty years. I was to be the first emissary from the family in America. This was really quite momentous for all of us.

I recently re-read all of the postcards that I sent home during the two months of our trip. When my mother passed away in 2013, my sister came across the packet of cards that my mother had saved all those years. It is remarkable that my dear mother collected all of the cards that I sent to my parents, my sister, my grandparents, and my aunt and uncle. I was amazed and delighted that she carefully saved them for me. I wrote a lot in those cards. They became another log of the trip because I attempted to describe so much of my experiences to the folks at home. There was one special card—to my grandfather—after I met his sister.

> *Dear Grandpa, We are now in Torino having a wonderful time. Today I met Amalia. She is wonderful and she sends*

her love. I can't wait to tell you all about it and show you pictures. This has been an emotional experience. Love, Anna

We arrived in Torino after leaving Rome and then drove up the western coast of Italy and on to Milan and finally Torino. On a hot July afternoon we found the apartment building on Via Giotti where the Fogliato family lived and we rang the bell. Through the intercom I simply said, "Amalia Marano," my grandfather's sister's name. I didn't know what else to say. Aware that we would be visiting at some point, the family had no idea of exactly when we might arrive. In a flash, Yolanda, Amalia's daughter, ran down the stairs and stood in front of us with open arms and ushered us into the elevator and back up to the apartment. The whole family was there—Yolanda and husband, Tony; their children, Teresa (eighteen), Tony (fifteen), Piera (twelve), and Aunt Beatrice and her husband—all excited as hell that *cugini* from America were visiting them. We didn't speak any Italian and they didn't speak any English, other than the little bit that Papa Tony had learned and remembered from when he was a prisoner of war in Australia during the Second World War. We learned that Amalia was spending the summer in the cooler mountains and that we would go to visit her the next day.

And they fed us! An Italian spread was laid out before our eyes. There was pasta, and eggplant, and chicken, and vegetables, and on and on and on. Ann and I were dazzled and we ate and ate and wanted to try it all. *Mangia! Mangia*! In my log I wrote, "Ann was like a pig in mud" with all of that *delizioso* Italian food. In and amongst all that glorious stuff was a plate of hotdogs, which we found odd and rather funny. We couldn't get over the fact that with all the other good and amazing Italian stuff that was offered, they wanted to watch us eat hotdogs!

They put us up for the night having to make adjustments in where they all slept to accommodate us. We went through masses of photographs of their family and of our family that my grandfather had sent to them over the years. Yolanda was my mother's first cousin and although they had not met one another at that point, you could tell how much having those photographs meant to the family overseas. And seeing photographs of Grandpa's siblings for the first time was an emotional experience for me. This was our heritage—our bloodline. It was such a tremendous experience for us—for me in particular, but also for Ann who could never have imagined anything quite like this. She was awestruck. This was nothing like her family.

The next day we jammed into the little blue family Fiat—Papa Tony the driver, Ann and I, and the three Fogliato children, Teresa, Tony, and Piera. I'm really not sure how far we drove to the mountain home where Amalia was staying, but it was quite a voyage. Up the steep mountain we climbed as Tony continuously beeped the horn to warn oncoming cars that we were coming the other way. (Italians are notorious for beeping car horns. Driving in the big cities is crazy and loud!) Ann and I kept looking back at one another with wide eyes as we noticed with fright how close we were to the humungous drop at the side of the road and thought, *Yikes! God help us!*

But we got there and we found Amalia. I was dumbstruck at meeting her. Here was a woman standing in front of me who was the spitting image of my grandfather. She was wonderful—so loving and so happy to have finally met someone from her brother's life in America. Powerful stuff. This was huge. It was a moment in time that I will never forget. In a way I had brought our entire family to her. And I was going to be able to share this

My great aunt, Amalia Marano and I

with the folks at home upon my return. It made me feel very special in a profound way. We spent the afternoon with Amalia and then traveled back to the city.

After another fun evening and overnight with the Fogliato family, we headed off once again and were on our way to Switzerland.

Amalia Marano and Fogliato family with me on veranda

I have to say that the time spent in Torino was an experience of a lifetime. I couldn't have understood beforehand what an impact it would have on me, nor would I have ever imagined how much their family would become part of my family's life in the future. The rest of our European trip was as fantastic as the first weeks that led up to our Torino visit, but nothing was going to compare to the warmth and love we felt in that apartment on Via Giotti.

Deepening the Love of a Country

My second trip to Italy wasn't until twenty-two years later in 1989 when my daughter Leigh turned thirteen years old. It was our special time together. It had been a long time since my first visit to Italy. I was a little timid about venturing out on my own and driving throughout the country. Because of that I decided to book a tour and leave the planning and driving to professionals. I chose a TWA tour that began in Rome and ended in Milan. The trip engaged the Italian railway system to transport us from city to city. We arrived in Rome and stayed in that beautiful city for a few days. While still at our hotel in Roma we took a short bus ride to Naples and then a ferry over to the enchanting island of Capri where we visited the Blue Grotto via small boats. It is an enthralling sight. From Roma we traveled to Florence (*Firenzi*) and did tons of sightseeing there. At thirteen Leigh was not very inclined to spend a great deal of time in museums, churches etc., and I had done all of that before. Instead, we shopped! Especially at the outdoor market in Firenzi. We treated ourselves to gorgeous genuine Italian leather jackets and we also purchased a beautiful attaché case for Leigh's attorney father. And we bought GOLD on the bridge that crossed the Arno—earrings, bracelets, and gold chains. We were typical tourists, and we loved every minute of it.

After Firenzi we traveled by train again to Venice (*Venezia*). All of our hotels on the trip were fantastic, but our hotel in Venezia was particularly spectacular. I enjoyed being back in Venice and I was very glad that I had chosen the type of trip that I did. It worked out quite well for us. The other folks on the tour were very nice and fun to be with. The group consisted of only twenty-four people from various places in the U.S. We specifically enjoyed two sisters from New York and spent a great deal of time with them. The older sister had attended my high school in Yonkers although a few years before my time. They were on a celebratory trip following terrible tragedies in each of their lives. They both endured very difficult times in the year prior to their trip to Italy and they wanted to give one another something to remember. We were honored to be there to help them heal by having fun in Italy with them.

Following several days in Venezia we boarded the train to Milan. We were on a two-week tour and we were to fly home from Milan. Cousin Piera drove from Turin to Milan to meet up with us on our last night in Italy. She arrived shortly after we checked in to our hotel and she insisted that she take us out to dinner. What an experience! Piera is a take-charge kind of woman and when you have an Italian order for you in her own country something wonderful happens. She knew exactly what was GOOD and we had a very memorable meal.

Piera stayed in the hotel with us that night and then came to the airport the next day to see us off. A very adorable Italian guy, whom we had met on one of our tours around Florence, was at the airport. Piera and I insisted that Leigh, a very embarrassed young teen, have her picture taken with him. He was *bellisimo*! Piera also gave us gifts of chocolates and other Italian foodstuffs, but airport personnel would not allow us to take them on board the plane. What a shame.

Between 1967 when I was in Italy the first time and 1989 when I was there again, a good deal of interaction had taken place with Piera and our family. Piera was twelve years old in 1967 when I first met her. My parents made two trips to Italy in the late '70s/early '80s and another trip when Uncle Dick accompanied them after Aunt Diane passed away. During those trips they spent considerable time with Piera's family. Both my grandfather and his sister, Amalia, passed away in the early '70s, transferring the relationship to the younger generation.

Before her grandmother died, Piera promised Amalia that she would learn English in order to continue to communicate with her American cousins and keep the relationship alive. She did just that. She studied English at school and expanded her knowledge of the language through her work. She eventually became a human-resource professional at a major aeronautics company—one that was affiliated with Boeing in the States. Her facility with English equipped her with a great asset in her job, and there was a time when she contemplated a transfer to the States. Piera continued to write to her American relatives on a regular basis and she even communicated with my grandmother's side of our Italian family. She served as the conduit for all communication and helped my mother with the translation of the letters she received that were written in Italian from all of the relatives in Italy.

After my parents' trips to Italy, Piera delighted us by booking a trip to the States. She flew to New York and my parents hosted her throughout her stay on this side of the Atlantic. Besides visiting family in New York, they also drove to Washington, DC, and then on to Martha's Vineyard in Massachusetts where my family was at the time. It was wonderful to see her in our environment, and that is when she met my family, including my children, David and Leigh.

The trip with Leigh in 1989 became the first of many other times that followed when we reconnected with Piera in Italy. And, no doubt about it, I was getting more hooked on Italy and what it meant to me. Frankly, I think that somehow Leigh's fascination with everything Italian was triggered by our Italian adventure in 1989. Little did we know then just how much!

More Travels to Italy

Two trips to Italy followed my excursion with Leigh and those trips were with my first husband, Keith, in 1997 and 1998. My married life was not complete bliss at that time, but I was still trying my damnedest to make it work. *"Let's go to Italy! Just the two of us. For our twenty-fifth anniversary!"*

I planned the entire trip. I wanted to go to different places—locations in Italy that I had not seen before. And I wanted Keith to experience Italy in a different way. We decided to rent a car and drive throughout the country and be free to roam at our own pace. We flew in and out of Milan. We went up to the Lakes first, Lake Como and Lake Menaggio, and stayed in Menaggio, and loved it there. We took the ferry over to Bellagio—one of the most beautiful spots in all of Italy. We sat in outdoor cafes, ate some outrageous food, and sipped lovely Italian wines—reminiscent of our honeymoon in the Greek Isles twenty-five years prior.

From the lakes area we drove to Venice, parked our car and spent several days in a very lovely small hotel on one of the canals off of San Marco Square. We strolled through the back streets of Venice, away from the canals and bridges, and rambled through the neighborhoods and gardens—areas that many tourists and visitors miss completely.

We traveled on to Florence and spent a few days in that beautiful city taking in the usual sights—the Uffizi, the Arno Bridge, Piazza Michelangelo, etc. We then spent a quiet and pleasant time in Tuscany where we stayed in the small town of Berino in a small farmhouse that had been renovated as a bed and breakfast. Those were a delightful few days. I loved everything about it. It was very pastoral and beautiful and it represented the epitome of Tuscan charm. The innkeeper had recently given birth to a baby girl and it was there that I learned of the Italian custom of placing a circular ribbon on the front door after the birth of a child—pink or blue.

During our stay in Berino I walked every morning about two miles along the country roads to the next small town of Montemoro. I drank in the scenery as well as the smells and vibrancy of the countryside and surprisingly even got a few nods from some of the locals. (If you have ever seen the movie *Under the Tuscan Sun,* you will know how significant a nod from a local can be.) I particularly noted the masses of tomato plants in each garden (at that time of year in May they were at their peak) looking a vibrant red—ready to be plucked off the vine. One could almost taste them. I also noted the roses in the front gardens of the houses in the village. They were the same red and pink roses I remember as a child at Grandma's house.

That area of Tuscany is where Chianti Classico comes from. We found several local restaurants and drank some very special local wines. We loved exploring and finding little hidden-away treasures and extraordinary restaurants. It was the first time I ever tasted the local peasant dish of Ribilletto. I absolutely loved it. It is made with day-old Italian bread, which is cubed and soaked in extra-virgin olive oil and then cooked with fresh tomatoes. The texture and aroma were winners with us. As soon as I returned home I attempted to make my own version of the dish. Good stuff.

Our anniversary was May 27th, and our two-week trip was planned around that time. The weather was perfect and spring is the perfect time to be in Italy, prior to the massive crowds of tourists that invade Italy during the summer months. We enjoyed driving through the countryside through small towns, and even loved driving on the Italian *autostrada* with its fantastic *Autogrills* where the freshly cooked food was just as good as in some of the restaurants. We liked being on our own. Keith was good at taking charge and exploring in unknown regions. Although I had meticulously planned the trip, we left enough time open for further exploration and adventure. Kit also took lots of pictures, which made me happy. Photography had been an interest of his way back in the early days of our marriage and I was pleased to see him reignite that interest to some degree.

The final days of the trip were spent driving back up north and stopping in Torino to visit Piera. Kit had met Piera when she came to the Vineyard in 1988. At the time she was living with Dominic, her boyfriend and partner, in their lovely apartment filled with antiques. Dominic was an antique dealer and it was so interesting to talk with him about his business. Sadly Piera and Dominic broke up after many years together. Theirs was not to be a lasting romance. He behaved miserably toward her—took all of the antiques and stripped their apartment after she had paid for most of it and left her to reboot her life. We were all heartbroken for her. Piera has said to me many times in her lilting English with her Italian accent, *"Annie, I am not lucky in love!"*

Notwithstanding what followed for both Piera and me with our relationships, the four of us had a lot of fun together and we enjoyed the visit tremendously. Then it was back home to Boston from Milan.

Did it help? Maybe. Keith and I enjoyed our trip. And we both loved Italy. If nothing else, it gave me a different taste of Italy and I was pleased to have planned a successful journey for us. It also made me appreciate the country of my ancestors all the more and realize that there was much more to learn about and experience in Italy. It wouldn't be long before I was back there again.

Same Trip–Year Later

And so we were going back to Italy again the very next year! My husband and a dear old friend had been involved in a real estate transaction from an investment they made way back in

1970—before I even met Kit. The whole deal was fraught with major complications over the years—many ups and downs and lots of difficulty with two other partners. As it evolved Kit and Gerry bought the other two partners out and Kit, the Boston attorney, handled all of the legal work involved with the deal. The O'Neills and the Vincolas determined that if the deal ever came to fruition and a substantial profit made, we would celebrate by taking a trip together. We were not in the habit of traveling with others, but this was different. Italy was our destination. And early October was the time frame. And once again I was entrusted with planning it.

Since our trip the previous year was so successful and we enjoyed the stops we made so much, we decided that doing about the same type of trip would be a good idea. The O'Neills had never been to Italy so they gave us the responsibility of the itinerary and the details. We flew in and out of Milan again and rented a car there. Kit did all of the driving and the O'Neills were very happy to sit in the back seat and let us take over.

We had an unfortunate experience at the airport, however. Gerry's luggage and my luggage was lost! It was nowhere to be seen. We left the airport in Milan, sans bags, and drove to the Lakes and stayed at the hotel in Menaggio where we had been the year before. I felt very comfortable in that little town and at that hotel. We remained there four days and as soon as we got there we began calling *Al Italia* about our lost bags. We fully expected that the airline would deliver them to us at the hotel momentarily as they promised. That never happened. Gerry and I were so frustrated that we were forced to shop for some clothing items—especially underwear. And since the October weather started to get a little chilly, I wanted a sweater. No luggage ever materialized at our hotel.

Cugina Piera to the rescue. I began telephoning Piera about our dilemma and she promised to get on the case. If you ever want anything done in Italy, Piera Fogliato is your go-to lady. She is persistent and demanding. And she gets action. After the four days in Menaggio concluded with no luggage, Piera finally confirmed that our bags were indeed at the airport in Milano, and that we could stop at the airport and pick them up before we headed east to Venice. Despite the lack of proper clothing, although Janet and Kit were just fine, we spent a lovely four days in that very beautiful region enjoying exceptional weather. We ferried over to the town of Bellagio across the lake a few times for some unforgettable meals.

On to Venezia. We parked the car and traveled by *vaporetto*—the mode of transport through the canals—to our hotel and enjoyed several days exploring San Marco Square and the Rialto Bridge areas. Food and meals became the highlight on this trip. Finding new restaurants, experiencing new tastes, and exploring the food markets became a daily activity. We did do some of the regular touristy things, but eating was our best adventure. Mind you, this was before "Trip Advisor" or "Yelp" sites to help one find a restaurant. We had fun searching for and making our own selections.

We took the vaporetto over to Murano to the glassworks and delighted in watching the glassblowing. The stop at Harry's Bar to drink and savor their famous *Bellinis* was also a highlight. And Janet and I were so excited to buy our knockoff Prada bags on the streets around the Grand Canal—before the police invariably chased the vendors away.

We made a quick stop in Florence and then it was on to Tuscany where we spent the remainder of our fifteen days in Italy. Once again we retraced the steps that Kit and I had taken the year before and even stayed at the same farmhouse in Berino. I do love all of Tuscany. We drove to Cortona and spent a day in the city of *Under the Tuscan Sun* by Frances Mayes, and also spent a wonderful day exploring the walled city of San Gimignano. Gerry could never quite pronounce *Gimignano* properly and I needed to correct him constantly. It became a recurring chuckle between us.

On the way back to Milano to catch our flight home we made arrangements to see Piera again and introduce our very Irish friends to our fiery Italian *cugina*. Piera came to Milan and met us at our hotel. Gerry and Janet were blown away by the experience of meeting Piera. Never had they been in the company of such a dynamo Italian woman who could talk and gesture to beat the band.

All in all, it was a very pleasant trip. And for the first time ever traveling with another couple, it went quite smoothly. What it did for me was to give me yet another look at this beautiful country and its gorgeous warm and friendly people . . . and taste the splendid food again!!! And make me crave more. At the same time these trips made me realize again and again that my Italian background meant something—it was ingrained in me, and I liked everything about that feeling. My visits to Italy made me aware that it was important to celebrate my heritage.

Finding Our Roots

In 2002 I had the pleasure of spending more time in Italy with my daughter Leigh. That excursion was perhaps the most significant of all my travels to *bella Italia* in terms of researching our roots and finding out more about our Italian heritage. And all the credit goes to Leigh. She was the one who started researching my father's side of the family. Throughout my childhood it was my mother's side of the family that played the most predominant role in all of our lives and little was known about the Patavinos' life in Italy before my grandfather Michele Patavino left his home country.

Leigh became enchanted with her Italian heritage and wanted to learn as much as she could. She began speaking with her Grandpa about his family and a stronger bond between the two of them emerged as a result. Dad even began speaking some Italian, which he had long forgotten and Leigh began studying the language herself. Leigh wanted to do what she could to give her Grandpa a better connection to his family and his family's history. As she did that her own interest in everything Italian grew. Later on she even had the opportunity to get to Italy on some work-related excursions within the food industry as she embarked on that aspect of her career. She learned what she could from my dad about his family, but that was minimal at best. All he knew was the name of the town where his parents lived in the Campobasso region of Molise and his mother's maiden name—Maria Micone from Montelongo, Italy. Leigh's Internet research led her to Marco Micone, originally from Montelongo, and now a resident of Montreal, Quebec.

Simultaneously, Leigh decided that she would plunge into another adventure of her own and she signed up for a second stint as a WOOFER (Willing Workers on Organic Farms) in Italy. She departed for Italy in February of 2002. Prior to that departure she continued her research for her grandfather and began a dialogue with Marco Micone. She learned that Marco is an accomplished playwright, teacher, and translator. Marco told us that his grandfather, Giuseppe Micone left Montelongo and immigrated to Canada, and that he continued to return to Montelongo throughout his lifetime, occasionally bringing Marco along as well. From that experience as a child and as a young man, Marco learned to love the little village of Montelongo too. His grandfather played a principal role in Marco's life and consequently Montelongo figured in Marco's life. He still maintained the house where my grandmother was born and he vacationed there with his family each year in August when all of Italy vacations.

Marco became a central figure in the plans that followed both for Leigh and then for me. We each talked with him on the phone several times and he was charmingly curious about our conviction that we were related. He offered his Montelongo home to us—if we were so inclined to make a visit there. He told us that his aunts, Peppinella and Loretta (on his mother's side), had the key to the house and that they lived near the fountain in the center of the tiny mountain village. They would welcome us.

Leigh left the States to begin her WOOF jaunt and spent a month working on farms in the Le Marche region; then she committed to a longer assignment at an *ecotourismo* farm outside of Siena. Simultaneously, she continued a dialogue with Marco, as did I. And also, simultaneously, I was preparing to leave on a trip to England for some antique buying for my shop on Martha's Vineyard. I was initially to spend a week touring the environs of London with a group of fellow antique-shop owners and then our Italy plan emerged. The plan was for me to travel by train from London to Pisa and meet up with Leigh prior to her joining her engagement in Siena and then we would proceed together to Molise on the Adriatic coast and search our roots there.

Leigh arrived in Pisa the night before me, secured a hotel, and rented a car. We were good to go. From the moment she picked me up at the train station, it became an unforgettable trip and so much was to lie ahead for both of us. Leigh, who is a writer by profession, penned a wonderful piece about that entire trip which, to my mind, captures all of the magic. In fact, I included that piece as an Afterword in my book, *Reunited: When the Past Becomes A Present.*

We left Pisa the next day and started traveling east. We reached Assisi that evening and we decided to stay there overnight. That experience in itself was memorable and we began having so much fun just being together and discovering new horizons. Leigh did all of the driving and I was extremely grateful for that since it was a challenge to drive on those mountainous roads and climb to the top to each town or city. Driving in Italy is challenging no matter where you go and I was so happy to let Leigh do all of the driving.

Leaving Assisi we drove south along the Adriatic coast. It was March and still felt like winter in that area of the country. The resort hotels along the coast were boarded up and it looked uninviting and surreal. We weren't quite sure of our next step. As we got closer to Montelongo, the town where my paternal grandparents hailed from, we began discussing whether we were really going to stop there and attempt to find Marco's aunts and find his house—or just find somewhere else to spend the night. The evening hours were closing in on us. We obviously needed to make a decision—quickly! There was NOTHING along the way that offered the remotest possibility. And then the sign for Montelongo appeared and we took a sharp right turn. We climbed to the top of the mountain in our little rented Fiat to the center of the village and looked for the fountain that Marco had described to us.

We were so unsure of ourselves. Leigh had gained some proficiency with her Italian and she approached a group of older men standing across from the fountain and asked them where we might find Peppinella, Marco's aunt and the holder of the key. Interestingly enough a slight little Italian woman had been standing at her front door just across from us, watching this encounter very intently. And the men pointed over to her. We parked the car in front of the house and entered. Peppinella knew exactly who we were; as thankfully, Marco had prepared the sisters of our potential arrival in Montelongo.

What followed for us were five days of remarkable adventures and lasting memories that notably impacted our lives.

During our stay in Montelongo we fell in love with Marco's aunts, Peppinella and Loretta and Loretta's son, Peppino. They treated us like royalty. They welcomed us into their home, cooked for us, and considered us family. Peppino became our chauffeur. After he settled us into Marco's home (incredibly the house where my own grandmother was born) and supplied us with the all-important bottle of home-pressed extra-virgin olive oil and coffee, we looked around our surroundings and couldn't quite believe where we were. It was chilly and the apartment seemed a bit dreary. We walked through the rooms and found blankets and bed linens, but our first night there was pretty cold. And the bathroom was downstairs in what was really the basement (originally where animals were kept) with a very tiny bathtub. It was all very interesting to we *Americanos*. Marco had warned us "it was not the Hilton!" The following night Peppino brought us a space heater, which helped a lot.

The next day Peppino took us to outdoor markets in surrounding towns to buy fresh produce and then to the town cemetery filled with Micone relatives long deceased. He also took us to the *Municipicio* office (town hall) which became key to the understanding of my father's background. The official there, Antonio DeMichele, helped us to find my grandparents' birth certificates, their marriage certificate, and the birth certificates of my two uncles who were born in Montelongo before the family traveled to the U.S. We also learned that my Uncle Patty was not the first Pasquale Patavino. Another baby had been born a year or two before him and that baby's name was also Pasquale Patavino. The family had never spoken of this. No one knew.

On our final day in Montelongo Peppino drove us to the city of Termoli on the Adriatic coast, a town about thirty minutes from Montelongo. It was there he introduced us to Zia Maria, then ninety-five years old, and the oldest living relative of the family. Peppino felt that if anyone could remember my grandmother and that generation of the Micone family, it would be Zia Maria. After a good deal of confusion and some rolling eyeballs and giggles between Leigh and I, there was an "aha" moment and Zia Maria confirmed that we were related!

It was all thrilling, humorous, and genuinely beautiful. For me it was incredible to be in the very home where my grandmother lived and to look out onto the hills of the beautiful countryside and imagine what life was like for them so many years ago. It was the experience that truly led to the desire to learn more about our heritage and pursue becoming citizens ourselves. Following our departure from Montelongo and the warm embraces from the two Italian women, Leigh and I continued on for a few more days in Tuscany and then it was time to say goodbye as I returned home to the States and she continued with her work on the farm in Siena. It became a time together that will remain with us forever—mother and daughter sharing a precious life experience.

The seeds were sown on this trip. We brought back his mother and father's birth certificates and his parents' marriage certificate to my father. The following Christmas Leigh presented her grandfather, Carmen Anthony Patavino, with beautiful framed pictures of the town in Italy where his mother and father were born. All of this was quite monumental and it meant so much to him. Dad passed away in July of 2003. My daughter gave him such a loving gift—the gift of knowing more about his mother and father's beginnings. Leigh hangs the pictures she gave him that Christmas along with portraits of his mother and father in her home to this day.

Italy With Alan

Alan and I were married on March 13, 2010, in Charleston, South Carolina. We didn't take a honeymoon then; rather we decided to wait until November to travel and Italy was our destination. Concurrently, my daughter, Leigh, had been making some major life decisions. She had been seriously contemplating leaving her job and moving to Italy. As it happened our trip and her plan coincided. Leigh also began to investigate how to apply for dual citizenship. The three of us were on our way to Italy and to become Italian citizens.

We contracted with Peter Farina of *ItalyMondo*, a company established to help Italian-Americans research their heritage and secure an Italian passport. As Leigh began the process, Peter suggested that I could easily do likewise as the paperwork would be the same. Then Alan realized that he qualified, too, through Grandpa Votta who was born in Venafro, Italy. The plan then became the triple purpose of a honeymoon trip, establishing residency in Italy for the purpose of applying for dual citizenship, and Leigh's search for work and a new life in Italy.

With Peter's help we rented an apartment in Termoli, Italy (in the Compobasso region where we filed our applications) and rented a car that we picked up in Rome once we arrived in Italy. Tickets purchased—we left together and flew out of Boston to Rome on *Al Italia*.

This trip was special in so many ways. It is hard to describe the significance of it all. Alan diligently kept a diary of the entire trip, and in his very colorful way, he captured the essence of it. (See Alan's diary entries in the Afterword.)

In 2012 we had our second adventure in Italy—and once again it became the three of us together. Alan and I were in Italy for just a little more than two weeks, but they were glorious weeks. We did so much and we "lived" there with Leigh in her apartment in Ostuni, *La Cita Bianca*. And because she was so entrenched in her life there by then we were able to take advantage of all of her knowledge, her facility with the language, her car, her driving skills, and the places she knew because of her job with Southern Visions Travel.

We also flew to Italy at no cost through Alan's military connection as a retired veteran. We flew "Space-A" out of Jacksonville, Florida to Sigonella Navy Base in Sicily. After our arrival there and spending a few days on the base (which were wonderful), we flew from Catania to Bari where Leigh picked us up and got us settled in her lovely rented apartment in the heart of the city of Ostuni. It was summertime and we swam in the Adriatic and ate fabulous meals. We traveled further south to Lecce and stayed in a wonderful Airbnb home with Piera who had taken the train to Bari to meet up with us.

(Alan's diary entries will give you a much more detailed accounting of the trips in 2010 and 2012.)

We have not been back to Italy since that trip and every year as spring approaches we get nostalgic for everything Italian and everything we have experienced there. Let us hope that not another year passes before we are back to the land of our ancestors—coming "full circle" once again. We are currently planning a trip to Puglia for May 2019.

PART THREE

Our Connection to the Country of Our Ancestors

Becoming Italian Citizens

Does having an Italian passport make us more Italian? As second- and third-generation Italian-Americans, Alan and I and our children have searched for the authenticity of what being Italian means. Tracing one's family tree has become much easier because of websites like Ancestry.com and the availability of immigrant-ship manifests at the Ellis Island website that many have engaged in the process of "going back" just as we have. However, getting to the ultimate goal—an Italian passport—can be a tricky business indeed.

As mentioned before, we began collecting documents that would validate our Italian heritage in 2002 when Leigh and I were in Montelongo. By 2010 we were fully into the process and our upcoming trip would help clinch it. Through Leigh's investigation and research we ultimately contracted with Peter Farina of *Italy Mondo* to help facilitate the procedure. At his suggestion, since we were planning to take a trip to Italy later in the year and Leigh intended to remain there to look for work, we agreed to try Peter's new method of establishing residency in Italy and register over there. We had to collect all of the documents beforehand. That meant birth certificates, marriage certificates, death certificates and divorce decrees for everyone—grandparents, parents, spouses and even exes. Peter's company and his staff are the best at unearthing documents and leaving no stone unturned to come up with the precious pieces of paper. We had already located some of the documents, but we would not have been able to find everything we needed if it had not been for Peter and his staff. One needs to locate every certificate and secure an original copy from the city or town of origin for everyone within the familial line—in this case my paternal grandfather for Leigh and me, and his paternal grandfather for Alan. Alan was starting from scratch to search for his documents, so locating the necessary paperwork for him became more difficult and time consuming. It does take time for each one of those documents to appear and then everything needs to be "apostilled" or certified—plus all documents need to be translated into Italian. Believe me, waiting for the paperwork to come in and knowing that we were good to go was more than trying at times. We were not sure that we would have everything we needed until almost the day of our departure.

The final document we needed to locate was my father's birth certificate—or baptismal certificate as a substitute, because Dad was born at home and he never had an official birth certificate. We weren't aware of this until the very last minute and trying to locate his baptismal certificate from the church in the Bronx where he was baptized was not an easy proposition. The church itself no longer existed and all of the records had been transferred to another church years before. It took several phone calls to the church rectory, conversations and pleading with the church secretary, and waiting for the pastor to give his blessing to release the certificate—so that it was all "legit" as the Hispanic church secretary explained to me. There were some anxious moments, needless to say, and we had to laugh nervously many times during the waiting period. Finally everything was in place and we took off to see what awaited us on the other side of the pond.

Peter helped us so much along the way. We picked up our car in Rome and drove from Rome to Termoli where Peter had arranged an apartment rental for us. It was by coincidence that Peter's roots are also in Compobosso and Molise, like ours, and that is where he established his Italian *ItalyMondo* office. He met his wife, Mena, there and he now lives in Italy full time with Mena and his new son.

Mena (Peter's fiancee at the time) and Peter met us at our apartment and got us settled. We enjoyed a wonderful lunch with them at a restaurant in the center of town and Peter even went shopping with us to buy essentials and groceries. In the days that followed Peter assisted us in registering our residency at the *commune* in Compobasso (the first requirement), helping Leigh get her *permesso di soggiorno* in order to work in Italy and remain there before her passport came through, and introducing us to Michele Vitale, our lawyer in Italy who would make it all happen. Both Peter and Michele were fabulous to us and we enjoyed many pleasant hours with them. Michele was efficient at his job and he even managed to introduce us to the Mayor of Termoli. That was a treat. So all the paperwork was in and registered and the waiting began.

After spending the required two weeks in Termoli (we needed to rent the apartment for a month) we moved on to Florence. While we were in Molise and in the Compobasso region, we visited Montelongo again and visited with Peppinella and Loretta and Pepino. Alan was able to find his grandfather's home in Venafro and speak with an official at the *municipio* in that city. All in all, it was a very successful mission.

We were fortunate to have done all of this when we did. We were at the beginning end of the now-huge push to gain dual citizenship. Today it is a much more difficult undertaking and it can take five to ten years to complete, along with considerable expense. Although we may have started searching our roots in 2002, we didn't start the formal process of securing our dual citizenship until 2010. So, in essence, it took us only two years to get it done.

Today there are numerous websites and Facebook pages for people who want to get into the process, directing them to where they can find help and guidance in getting there. There are at least three sites that I monitor on Facebook; *Dual US-Italian Citizenship*; *ExPats in Italy*; and *Americans Living in Italy*. They all offer Americans assistance from the very beginning of their research to the final step in securing an Italian passport. Every time I read a post I am totally amazed at how arduous a task it has become and how much more difficult it seems.

It is possible for Americans to do everything on one's own without contracting with a company that specializes in the process, but it is very difficult, and I wouldn't advise it. It can take up to five years to get an appointment at some consulates, as well as secure all of the necessary documents. Some consulates in U.S. cities are notorious for being difficult and the wait for an appointment can take forever. Most consulates schedule appointments two years out, and often there are postings for appointments that people canceled if they are not ready with all of their documents. In other words, today the ordeal is totally different than it was for us when we started in 2010 and the cost can be upwards of $10,000 and can take up to ten years—a very frustrating ten years. We are so glad that we completed everything when we did.

Italy granted citizenship to more than 200,000 people in 2016. That's a big number! Mind you, not all of those people obtained their citizenship through their heritage, but it is the easiest way to get to the end result. For Americans the three ways of obtaining Italian citizenship are 1) you have Italian parents or grandparents; 2) marry an Italian; 3) go native, or stay in Italy for more than ten years providing you obtain a *permesso di soggiorno*. All three methods can be a bureaucratic nightmare.

The key to qualifying for Italian citizenship, i.e., Jure Sanjuinis ("to the blood") is that you have to prove either that the ancestor you are applying through did not become a U.S. citizen before the next person was born in your line of ascendants, or that they never became a citizen at all. And that can be the tricky part with birth dates coming in to play as well. Today EU nationals can live in Italy permanently without as much as a visa, and non-Europeans also have the option to stay without acquiring citizenship, thanks to Italy's permanent residency permit or *carta di soggiorno*. That's what Leigh had to apply for when she first arrived in Italy in 2010 intending to stay and work there.

The wait to hear that everything was approved in Italy for us took approximately a year and a half. We finally heard that our application was approved and we received the apostilled documents in April of 2012. We scheduled an appointment at the Italian Consulate in Miami, Florida, for the beginning of May. Since we lived in Sarasota, Florida, at the time, Miami was the consulate we needed to go through. We drove to Miami with friends from home and spent the weekend there. It was an event.

Our appointment went as smoothly as possible. We paid the requisite fees and were told that our passports would be in the mail within two weeks. And they were! Our Italian passports were issued May 30, 2012, and will expire May 29, 2022. We traveled to Italy on June 30, 2012 with our Italian passports in hand. It is ironic that even though she started the whole process and she was living in Italy at the time, Leigh's passport did not come through until months later.

We like to think that having that legal document makes us a little more Italian and brings us a little closer to our Italian ancestors. Whether or not we will enjoy other benefits of our Italian passports in the future, only time will tell.

Cultural Differences Between Italians and Americans

All things considered, what makes someone Italian? Is it their heritage? Is it how often they've traveled to Italy or lived there? Or is it something else?

A Pew Research study conducted in 2017 found that "learning the language" was the key factor in becoming Italian and was the most critical to national identity regardless of birthplace or birthright. And that is the reason why I intend to continue the arduous task of becoming somewhat fluent in Italian. I have a long long way to go!

There are decidedly other things that contribute to making one Italian or not. There are numerous cute lists that start off with "You're Italian if. . . ." that make sense to those of us who embrace being Italian. I've always enjoyed seeing how many of them fit in with me and my family and my lifestyle.

Some of the differences that seem to make Italians more unique than Americans or other nationalities are rather endearing

I think, although they can also be rather annoying, too. One is that Italians almost always talk loudly. "I'm not yelling; this is my normal voice," is a statement heard over and over again. And, of course, Italians gesture with their hands—and arms—to make a point. I am very guilty of this one.

Another very Italian-ism is their emotional response to everything. Italians wear their heart on their sleeve and cry a lot, whether it is showing happiness or sadness. And that goes for men as well as women. Sometimes Italian men seem more emotional than Italian women, and they can cry at the most seemingly insignificant time.

The importance of meals and sharing of food is another very Italian thing. The vision of an Italian mama cooking for her family and saying, "*mangia, mangia*" is a familiar one to Italians and non-Italians alike. Having a spread put forth before you after just stopping in to say hello is a very common occurrence. And the timing of meals is uniquely Italian as well. In Italy the afternoon meal is usually the main meal. The workday stops at around one o'clock in the afternoon and family and friends gather for a nice meal, after which everyone disperses to home for *riposo*—the mid-day naptime. I always found that so civilized and welcome while in Italy, especially during the hot summer months. It just makes sense to me—and I do like an afternoon nap! In Italy the shops and offices all close during the hours of one to five and then remain open until eight in the evening, at which point everyone begins to think about another meal. Italians don't eat dinner until nine or ten o'clock at night. Again, all of this seems to fit more into my habits and lifestyle. At home I find that I am often not starting to make dinner until eight or nine o'clock. I guess, for us, it may not be the healthiest approach, but I like it.

Coffee habits are uniquely Italian—*Café, Espresso, Cappuccino*—and when to drink them. All Italians start their day with a strong cup of café made in their simple *Moka* or more elaborate coffee maker. After living in Italy and coming back to the States, Leigh got used to bringing her *Moka* and other coffee paraphernalia along with her wherever she went. And in Italy coffee bars seem to be on every corner, where Italians meet and greet one another and stand at the bar for their morning café or cappuccino. Italians drink cappuccino up to ten o'clock in the morning with their usual *cornetto*, but never later in the day and definitely not at nighttime. I am always amazed when I hear someone order a cappuccino after a meal in an American restaurant. Definitely not an Italian thing! Espresso is the drink for nighttime. Americans are so concerned with consuming too much caffeine, but that doesn't seem to bother Italians at all. A strong espresso seems to be me to be the perfect end to a delicious meal and I do enjoy one from time to time—especially when I am in Italy. And for some reason it never gives me a headache—when I'm in Italy, that is.

Another aspect of Italian life is their "*a domani*" attitude about most things, meaning "don't worry; leave it for tomorrow." Theirs is a more relaxed approach to life's inconsistencies, often at odds with their emotional outbursts over simpler things. It can be humorous, and it can be frustrating to say the least, especially when it comes to getting things done, say at the bank or the post office or other official business that might become necessary. Standing in long lines is something that Italians get very used to, and one might need to return several times to finalize some important business. It is very much a part of their way of life.

At the same time Italians are notable for their ability to "do nothing" called *Dolce far Niente*. It is not uncommon to see someone just standing or sitting for the longest time seeming to not have a care in the world and just enjoying the moment. To me, I think that we should all take more moments like that and look around and stop and listen. Not a bad idea, if you ask me.

Italians may like to do nothing at times, but they like to drive their cars—FAST, with no mind to signs or speed limits. Driving in a city in Italy is a very challenging ordeal—with cars and motor scooters dashing in and out of the smallest spaces. It is noisy and it is confusing, and trying to find a parking space can be downright impossible. When Leigh lived in Italy she learned to drive just the way Italians do. We were totally amazed at her prowess and her daring—and so glad that she was doing all the driving and getting us from place to place.

The last thing I want to mention about "Italians being Italian", is that Italians are famous for their long goodbyes. In any Italian household, whether it be in America or in Italy, saying goodbye to family members takes forever. There is the goodbye in the kitchen; the goodbye in the dining room; the goodbye in the living room; the goodbye at the front door; and even the last goodbye at the car driving off. And there are more kisses and hugs—*baci et abbracci*—at every stop. That was most certainly my experience in the house at 326 North High Street in Mount Vernon, New York. We called them "Marano Goodbyes." It could take another half hour or hour for us to finally leave after Sunday dinner. There was always something else to say or go back to do. We laughed at ourselves, but we genuinely hated to say goodbye.

And that is the reason that I have taken the time and effort to write all of this because I have hated to say goodbye and I don't want to lose the memories of a beautiful time in my life and the beautiful people who made it so.

What makes one Italian? It's the people—and the love they have for one another.

And it is family—la famiglia—as I've mentioned before. I hope that both my immediate family, as well as my extended family, appreciate what our ancestors have given us and that my efforts at memorializing some of the past gives us all a better understanding of our heritage. My generation and the generations of our children and grandchildren benefited greatly from our grandparents' lives and experiences. We have been blessed with the beautiful gifts they bestowed upon us and we proudly continue with the traditions of our Italian-American culture.

And now, please enjoy my husband Alan's diary entries of our fun trips to Italy in 2010 and 2012.

Afterword

Diary Entries by Alan Votta

ITALY—OCTOBER 30, 2010 TO DECEMBER 2, 2010

10-30-10

Depart Charleston 10:30 AM. Arrive Boston 3 PM. Joined up with Leigh in terminal at Logan airport as if we were a precision choreographed dance troupe. After a wonderful greeting and smiles and kisses, we proceeded to our check-in. We departed on time and enjoyed a very nice flight from Boston to Rome. (One negative note was that we had the only passenger with his overhead light on during our appropriate sleep time sitting right behind us!!)

Arrived Rome. Customs was a "bear"! Ha! Stamp passport and go!!! Ravage countryside! NO scrutiny at all. I guess that's Italy for you.

Because of jet lag/no sleep and change in general, we picked up our car rather wearily. I was grateful that Leigh took up the task of driving. I could not consider it. I was so tired! I could have been more of a liability than an asset behind the wheel.

We found our apartment in Termoli and eventually met up with Peter, Filomena and Michele. Terrific initial encounter—all parties were amiable and delighted to finally meet and start our process. The apartment was much better than any of us had thought possible. The three of us went to lunch with Peter and Fil. Great fun was had by all; we went back to the apartment and the evening came to a complete halt for me. I brushed my teeth—that's all—and I crashed until well after sunup. The Adriatic apartment has a 180-degree water view, olive trees adjacent to parking lot and a view of Old Termoli. Originally we thought our area was new construction during the Mussolini era. Wrong! Where we had lunch was the Mussolini area and we are the new adjacent zone.

Ann and Leigh have been brainstorming (and agonizing) over getting cell phones up to snuff—including emails, texts, phones—and satellite connection with Obama! Of course I am relaxing and being strictly a voyeur. It is really like observing a Chinese Fire Drill. Very entertaining.

We finally broke loose from the apartment and ventured to the old walled part of the downtown area—Old Termoli. 5th century wall construction. One building of sorts, probably the highest point for visual spotting. The construction starts off in a pyramidal ascent—very unusual and very beautiful. Had a wonderful dinner to end the day.

11-2-10

Soon off to Compobasso to meet Peter. Big step, big day—dual-citizenship paperwork submitted to appropriate authority to establish residency. We met with Peter and had a successful day at the regional central offices of the Molise area of Italy. Very picturesque and quaint—reeking of history. After the business at hand was accomplished we all went to a wonderful restaurant in a small town, Bojano. The food was wonderful and we had a delightful time. Of course, we invited Peter to join us. He has become part of our extended family. We then commenced a weary ride home.

11-3-10

We awoke this morning and we all finally had our first successful "good" night's sleep. Jet lag and just general excitement, plus the newness and change of routine had had us all exhausted. This morning we are meeting with Michele (attorney to the stars and Peter's cohort in crime) to take care of legal matters. Michele is our lawyer and our link to city hall (*Municipio*) to register us as citizens of Termoli and part of our journey to become citizens of Italia. He is a very gentle man and we are confident with him as our advisor and advocate. He even introduced us to the Mayor of Termoli.

Then it was back home to our Termoli residence for our afternoon rest (*mezzogiorno*) like all good Italians do. The rest was good for all of us and we then headed back downtown to have an adventure and retrieve a cell phone we'd left behind at the Wind store to be charged. Leigh picked up some computer and electronic device so that she could get online and then it was off to have gelato. I chose to have hot cocoa. The gelato was delicious, but the cocoa was like drinking chocolate icing— somewhat loose. Enjoyed it, but never again!

Did I mention that last night we received word that Ann's air conditioner condenser had been stolen from the house in Sarasota?! And then tonight Ann's accountant created another fright needing to talk to her "right away"! When she did place the call, he said nothing seems to be urgent and that she could wait until our return. He scared the hell out of Ann and me, and then it wound up being a false alarm.

11-4-10

Drove to a nearby town called Camparo and then to their beach. It was of course, off-season so it was like a ghost town. In season it has to be very colorful. We did not venture too far on the beach. The weather was not very conducive. Back to Termoli and eventually back to downtown Termoli to join the procession of locals as they promenade up and down the main street in town—*passegiatta*. It was all very pleasant and then we went to have "pizza." It was a very good experience until we met an American couple. He was a GAG first class and the type that embarrasses fellow Americans. Onward to home after a very nice day.

11-05-10

Back to Compobasso to meet Peter again. He helped Leigh sign up for her Italian Social Security Card. This is perfect for her and her future Italian adventures. After formalities Peter suggested we ride to the top of the mountain to the castle of Compobasso. Back in the Fascist days Mussolini approved of turning the old fort into a mausoleum for the military men of Compobasso who'd been killed in World War I. The fort was in bad shape back then and a lot of reconstruction took place. It is very touching and beautiful and its majestic view is awesome. Peter then made us aware of a wonderful *trattoria* he knew about (a slow-food restaurant) and it was located in Montelongo! He called ahead for us and made a reservation that resulted in a greeting to be remembered.

The town is way up high in the clouds and so medieval. (Homes built when Columbus was getting his donkey permit. Teenager, you know!). Of course, the restaurant owner (a one-gal operation) knew Ann and Leigh's relatives and contact was made. After dinner a gentleman arrived (Loretta's son) and we became reacquainted with Marco Micone's aunts and what had transpired with them since 2002 when Ann and Leigh made their first visit to Montelongo. Before leaving the restaurant Leigh was taught how to make a local specialty pasta. We had one of the best meals ever at that restaurant. After leaving the restaurant we went to visit with Loretta whose residence had changed since the earthquake hit Montelongo in November 2002. Ann and Leigh were quite amazed at how different the town looked since their visit and were so sorry to see that Loretta and Pepinella's home was almost destroyed. It is uninhabitable now and they were relocated to new housing set up by the Italian government. Loretta was wonderful to us and she talked and talked in her Italian while none of us understood anything she was saying—even Leigh. We smiled and enjoyed ourselves and were pleased that Loretta pointed out the vase that Ann had sent as a thank-you from their visit in 2002. The vase made it through the earthquake!

We made it home and we were so exhausted. Leigh took a nap and I did the same. Ann stayed upright and I arose two hours later. Ann and I then chatted for quite a while until bedtime became obvious for me again and finally for Ann too.

11-6-10

Saturday and our plan is, like most days, less than strict. We will be heading toward Puglia (a region in the south) that is about a three-hour drive from Termoli. It should be flatter and maybe a little warmer. We are exploring the possibility of staying at a B&B in Ostuni and are excited about the prospect of seeing Puglia and what it has to offer.

So we are off on our adventure to Puglia to spend the night/weekend in timeless and immeasurable beauty. We slept the night in Ostuni (*La Cita Bianca*—the White City). Everything in this region is made of an abundant stone, quarried there, which I believe to be travertine. All is very thick and will be here long after man leaves this earth. Our rooms were the most beautiful caves the eye could behold. We poked around and had lunch, which was again, noteworthy.

11-7-10

After leaving the B&B off we went to explore the countryside and get close to one of the many wonders of this region—the *trulli*—small stone round structures with conical roof caps. They are all over the region by the hundreds. Folklore has it that when the taxman visited the property, the farmer would break down the trullo and argue that the trullo was just a pile of rocks and no more. Plus there was no mortar used in the building, hence it was tax-free! After the taxman departed the farmer would then reassemble his home. Still another yarn is that the number of cones on the structure indicated how many boy children the farmer had, which consequently made him the envy of the populace near and far.

At this point I feel compelled to say that my attempt at words to describe everything that we are experiencing and to tell the whole story is almost impossible to write. The adventure that Ann, Leigh and I are on is so deep and so moving; I fail to do it any justice. Leigh had started the ball rolling a long time ago, testing the possibility of dual citizenship and her desire to live in Italy. Many "winks" later, we three are about to become Italian citizens! Leigh doesn't quite know what to think of Ann and my take on "winks" and that there is not a coincidence that was not meant to happen in the first place. Some very powerful force directed Leigh, and Ann and I were destined to follow. Leigh has become instrumental in closing another long trip—a circle, as it may be. My father, and his years of genealogy pursuit, was never able to close one circle of information and that was Venafro, Italia. Tuesday, we three will be where my father has never been and I will be finishing his work; may he rest in peace knowing I/we have come and conquered Venafro the way he wanted to but trusted me to finish.

Late entry. We closed out the day at a "slow food" restaurant Ceglie Messipica, another astonishing town of untold beauty. The meal was superb. Ann had salted cod, Leigh had rabbit and I had donkey! (I am for some reason, looking for a hat that my ears can come up through the brim). The restaurant was visually everything you would want it to be in Italia. No words could describe it all. It was total sensual fulfillment.

11-8-10

A day of rest dictated by some inclement weather. Late in the day Pepino (from Montelongo) drove over to Termoli to see us and we went for a *passegiatta*. As it is and has always been in Italy, we then parted company for a couple of hours and regrouped late in the evening for another late meal—past 8 in the evening. That's what you do in Italy!

Pepino took us to a restaurant—for all intents and purposes, it was a "truck stop," and a place where the *polizia* frequent for their evening meal. We ordered (or Pepino ordered for us!) and we were astonished at the quantity of food presented to us—an appetizer to feed two as a complete meal. The second course was homemade seafood pasta—so delicious—and the main course was more fish—remember you are already stuffed. The main dish consisted of octopus, carp, baby squid and shrimp and langusto, plus a whole flounder—all grilled on a wood fire. *Bellissimo*! Add the wine, the bread and the Coca Cola. My fear was that I could not fold my body enough to get back into the car to head home. Home was accomplished and a fond memory and experience was had by all.

11-9-10

Off to Venafro! The ride was breathtaking, however Mother Nature stepped in and the worst day in Italy came upon us. We forged on and made it to Venafro. Grandpa told me it was on the side of a hill. The hill looked like Mt. Everest!

The streets were so tight and narrow, but cars ventured helter-skelter in and out of seemingly impossible alleys. The town

AFTERWORD

is ancient and the look is certainly of antiquity. We think of old as 200 or 300 years, but Grandpa's birthplace was built in the 1700s, and other structures were built in the 1400s. We found 2 Via Cavour. I knocked on a door and a young lady wearing chef's clothing appeared. Leigh, our interpreter, explained our/my plight and allowed us in at another door. We entered what had once been the cellar area and a working olive oil pressing area—-with the old press still in its original location. This nice lady and her husband were renting this level and they'd converted it into a "Pub"—a transformation of an old olive oil pressing factory into a luxurious bar/restaurant. Also apparent in the space was an ancient cistern that they cleaned out and illuminated, the circular olive press, two wheels that a donkey walked around in circles so as to cause the crushing. The nearby walls were modified so that the donkey's rounded belly would fit past the corners. An amphora of unknown age was on display behind ancient metal bars. The owners of the bar believe the area had not been used for more than 50 years. The upstairs two apartments had also been renovated and were currently being rented as subsidized housing.

    I felt good. I made the trip to Glasgow, Scotland to Dad's birthplace and now I have done the same with Grandpa's place of birth. I managed to locate the city of Venafro's "Town Treasurer" and had a *cafe* with him. He told me who to speak with at City Hall (*Municipio*) and I was able to gain some information. I looked through books that were ancient parchment and could glean only a snippet of information. Of course, Peter had done all of this for us and the information was well in hand for the citizenship. Dad would have had a ball! The experience I had was tremendous.

    We departed Venafro and I felt exhilarated. I felt good.

11-10-10

Sort of a laid-back day and we didn't do too much. We had a great lunch in the old section/old town of Termoli. We walked a bit around the Castello—a Frederick II design. Termoli is the closest point to a lot of Middle Eastern countries. A lot of black market and general mayhem enters Italy at this vantage point. You don't walk the beach at night—foot patrols and helicopter surveillance are apparent. One could get into a lot of trouble. We walked the beach in broad daylight with no ill side effects.

Home after dusk and had pizza from around the corner. And it was damn good!

11-11-10

We took a trip toward Compobasso stopping at a couple of different small towns and, of course, they are on top of hills that defy imagination. The first town we stopped in was not that impressive from an old-town-flavor perspective, but the view was spectacular. Impeccably kept farms, with vistas terminating at the Adriatic for at least 180 degrees around. That town was Montorio.

The next town we reached was Lorino—quite cosmopolitan and picturesque. We stopped and shopped for fresh veggies in a plaza. The farmer we dealt with treated us like old friends and he made the price right. Off to another town, a bit impromptu as we were satisfied thinking the day had come to a close early this afternoon. Leigh suggested that we try one other town and not much persuasion was needed. Off we went up and over more hills, but beautiful vistas all about. We witnessed people eating lunch while taking a break from work in the olive groves

AFTERWORD

(harvest time in Molise). The town was Porto Canoni. More olive groves and life all around. We then went into the town center and we noticed several farmers pulling trailers filled with olives. We toured the little town. It was sweet to say the least. On an impulse I tracked down where the farmers were going. They were heading to an olive growers' Co-Op. A gold mine of an adventure soon followed.

We parked the car and walked past numerous tractors in a long line waiting to have their olive harvest weighed and to dump their load. I approached a gentleman and after some fumbling, I managed to ask (with Leigh's help, of course) whether we could tour the facility. He smiled and we were given a tour of tours! We saw the entire cycle of "olives to olive oil." What a treat. I was allowed to climb on machinery to take better pictures from up close and closer still. We discovered that the gentleman I had approached initially came all the way from Naples to make a deal to purchase olive oil. He and Leigh swapped business information and a possible olive oil import/export alliance may have been made.

We then thought about trying to work out a possible trip to see Nando's operation near Naples in a town called Caserta. After purchasing some olive oil for ourselves and concluding our extended visit, we headed out of town, quite exhilarated by our experience at the Co-Op. On the way out of town while driving past thousands of olive groves, I spotted some activity. I parked the car and we all went into the fields and interrupted an old farmer with his hired help (Albanian husband-and-wife team) as they were gathering olives. The tractor was running to create the air necessary to activate a set of hard plastic rakes mounted at the end of a pole that opened and closed quite rapidly causing a fierce raking action. One pushes the device up into the branches of the tree and this causes all hell to occur. OLIVES raining down on you from multiple directions—many falling onto your head, face and body. The ground all the way around the base of the tree is covered in a green mesh. When a tree is considered harvested, the net is walked to the center where the olives are concentrated in large piles and then placed into trailers. Leigh and I had a ball. The farmer allowed us to operate the "rake." Pictures were taken and we left after many thanks were exchanged between us and the farmer and his helpers. It was certainly a wonderful wonderful day of fun and adventure.

11-13-10

We are on our way to Caianello near Caserta, and that is where Nando, our olive friend from the olive co-operative visit lives. We became very friendly and we were invited to his place of business that I, if not all of us, thought would be some kind of storefront. Not so. We linked up in a nearby business district and off we went into the beautiful Italian countryside. After a bit we entered a driveway and a very nice large home appeared. We were a little confused until Nando led us to the back of the house and a rather large structure loomed ahead of us and seeing trucks, trailers and other conveyances filled with olives, I became even more confused. We soon learned that Nando and his family have had an olive oil pressing business for more than 60 years and we were to be introduced to yet another experience that gave us real insight as to how olive oil is made. We had a

AFTERWORD

wonderful day and were treated to tastes of their olive oil as well as some of the best pizza we ever tasted!

11-14-10 — OFF TO NAPLES

What an experience Naples is! People all over the place! We parked in a parking garage and still had quite a trek to our B&B, a building that, 300 years ago, was for one of the Pope's right-hand men. It looked medieval and felt like Roman soldiers were going to suddenly appear. We were in old Naples and we poked around the shopping district that was prepared for Christmas— as far as the eye could see—Christmas, Christmas, and more Christmas. The sights and sounds were unbelievable and we all had a wonderful time. Food—GREAT.

We rested well that night and Monday we were back into the streets and folding in with the masses. Off to the Duomo of Naples. What a sight. At first a little unassuming; however, when you realize what a spectacular sight it truly is, I thought of my Dad more than once or twice. By noon we were on our way out of town heading back to Termoli. Great ride back. (After thought—We all agreed that the trip to Naples was well worth the effort—congested, but a must for all coming to Italia.)

We arrived back in Termoli a bit exhausted, but many new experiences carried the day. However, when we arrived back at the apartment—NO WATER! Ann made the right call and in an hour or two the problem was solved.

11-15-10

We met with Michele (the attorney) and the last stamps and administrative functions were applied to our packages. Many months of genealogy, birth and death certificates, divorce and marriage certificates, etc. had preceded this meeting. We thought we were coming to the end of the ordeal. Now our "packages" were in the hands of the Italian bureaucracy and now the waiting begins for what is truly a dream and an honor—citizens of Italia! The Patavino and the Votta name will be solidly bound to our Italian heritage. Big Deal/Big Day—one not to be taken lightly. Well worth the effort.

Next Leigh applied for her green card. This is to cover her extended stay in Italy. Italian citizenship finality will take longer than the time allowed on the current visit.

We extended our stay in Termoli and took Michele to have a cafe. Ironically, we bumped into his fiancee, and we all sat and had beverages and wonderful conversation.

We then went back to the apartment and closed out our last-minute tasks there and proceeded to prepare for our next adventure—FIRENZE! We got Leigh to her apartment, visited with her roomie and Ann and I were off to our little place. What a special special place. Talk about "to die for." What a setup. The house goes back to the 14th century. The ambiance is phenomenal.

A side note—DRIVING IN ITALY! It is like driving in a Chinese fire drill—or in a blender—or in a crowd and some fool throws out a hand full of money and the crowd is all in vehicles—OF ALL TYPES. Scooters are the worst. A book could be written on this subject quite easily.

The approach to the apartment is medieval at best. Cars drive where donkeys and cars have had difficulty. While approaching the residence I had to bob and weave—back up and squeeze hard left and hard right—in the dark, then let Ann out of the car and back up on an incline in a stick-shift French car! And then press it up against a 2000-year-old wall and not touch it, so there would be enough room to allow other cars to pass. Two rooms make up our apartment. Put some bars on the front door and it could be a DUNGEON.

We crashed soon after arriving in the apartment. We were bushed, beat and flat-ass tired!

11-16-10

We lingered in bed until early afternoon. We needed that time to recuperate and the BED—finally a BED. Proper size, sheets—real sheets and a comforter and blankets that created a most wonderful horizontal experience. Good for sleep too.

Shopping came next and it was a pleasant adventure.

11-18-10

Our day was one of self-indulgence. We did little or nothing. We needed the rest and are preparing for an evening out with Leigh at Zabibo—Benadetta's restaurant (Leigh's friend and restaurateur and author she has been working with). We picked up Leigh and off we went. Leigh's apartment is on a tight street and is always an adventure picking her up. Success and off to Benadetta's. GPS on the ready. After what seemed to be a lifetime of lefts and rights, we arrived at the restaurant. Very very nice and in short order we were meeting Benedetta and we were treated extremely well. After a lot of chitchat and laughter Benedetta ordered for us. One fine experience after another—eating experience that was pure delight. Good time had by all.

(Late entry). In this case we did not pick Leigh up at her apartment. Instead she walked to a landmark called Piazza de Michelangelo. It was raining on and off, but Ann and I had enough dry time to see a most spectacular sight. That is FIRENZI. It appears as it has for hundreds of years—no skyscrapers. What a view. You can see history and the Italian secret called love of country and *familgia*. Then the adventure of taking Leigh home again to *la cita centro*.

11-19-10

We three merry musketeers managed to get together for an outing—a trip to Cortona. Lovely, beautiful, and sights that defy description. We ate in a restaurant that was built around the time of Leonardo DaVinci. Everything is built of stone—massive stone and a lot of it. No fire department needed. There was so little to burn.

We then pressed on to Montepulciano. It was late and we did little more than a drive through. The drive was magnificent.

11-20-10

Ann awoke with quite a headache. We took it slow and did a little shopping and Federica, our hostess, suggested a restaurant up on the approach to Fiesole. We found the restaurant and the setting truly one of a kind. Our food once again was superb. And the best part of the experience was meeting the restaurateur—our newest BFF. I asked him at a point before really getting to know him, who he was in the scheme of things and I said that he looked like the kitchen help. It took him a while, but he finally came clean. He was the owner. From there we proceeded to have a great time with him. When trying to exit, he did not want us to leave, but we promised to come back. I also managed to tell him our story—Facebook and the whole ten yards! He enjoyed the story and presented us with a beautiful bottle of Florentine Chianti. We left with smiles on our faces.

Ann's headache is still very much a topic. We have to watch out for possible culprits.

11-21-10

The three musketeers—Ann, Leigh, and Alan—all mustered on to the top of Piazza de Michelangelo and then went off to Benedetta's again for Sunday brunch. What a mis-characterization! We were exposed to a treat—a glorious experience. Veal, pasta, eggplant parmesiano, turkey with a sauce to dream about, etc. etc.

We spent the better part of three hours visiting and eating and not feeling guilty at all.

The day came to an end. We deposited Leigh back home to her medieval fortress and we went on to our fortress in the hills.

11-22-10

Our plan today was to pick up Leigh and friend, Hillary, and be off to Lucca! The idea seemed simple—go into the heart of Firenze with a million cars and two million scooters and add 500,000 strange little vehicles that barely carry one human being—to pick them up. That meant finding a needle in a haystack. Leigh and Hillary would be waiting for us at the base of the bridge. OK. Now try doing all of this with every car, scooter, bus and strange contraption on the road pushing you out of the way and hanging on for dear life. Success? NO! Almost. Ann gets out of the car. I am at a bus stop. Ann says, "Move." And I do—not knowing where the hell I was going to go. No phone. No address. And no navigator. What do I do? I followed the GPS. Reset it, hopefully, and off I went on a merry journey around Florence—up to Piazza Michelangelo and down the hill back through Florence and amazingly back at my starting point—ready to kiss the ground. There was Ann. No girls?????? We parked in the middle of one of the bridges over the Arno and put on the emergency flashers and Ann is frantic trying to establish some sort of communication. Finally, after a lifetime slipped by, we were all present and accounted for and with my heart finally at rest, we were off to Lucca!

Lucca wound up being the antidote for the disastrous start to our day. It is beautiful. It has a history from Roman times through every upheaval in Italian history. Napoleon was in the mix. He basically owned Lucca at a point in time and gave it to his sister. She proved to be an asset adding many visual delights and a most charming two-and-a-half-mile walk on the promenade all the way around the city. We loved our day in Lucca even though we even managed to get lost! We never realized that we hadn't made a mental note of where we came into the city. Oh, my poor feet! To solve the problem, we climbed up to the top of the walled city ramparts and started walking to the right. We felt that we would HAVE to notice something—a landmark—and stop. Of course, we should have walked to the left. We almost walked the entire two and a half miles again before coming to our starting point. Ann's foot was killing her (plantar fasciitis), but we finally found the car and then I proceeded to try to break a leg or something else. After helping Ann into the car, I foolishly tried to walk across the front of the car where leaves and tree roots were hidden. I misjudged the situation and stepped on to a minefield of vegetation. And down I went onto my right side with a great thump. More embarrassed than anything else; I managed to rise with no visible fractures or blood. Sore as hell though. Life goes on.

11-23-10

We lazed the day away. More phone problems than I care to mention. When we finally connected with Leigh we learned that she was under the weather, so her day was limited. Our highlight was to go to a restaurant in our neighborhood and we literally killed three-plus hours having food that was so delightful and tasty. We knew we were in a good place when we realized we were lucky to get a table and saw the quality of the patrons. After the three-plus hours, we were forced to move on because the restaurant wanted to close. Siesta. They call it lunch. They close and don't reopen until 7:30 PM . The best part is how they get you out! They turn off the HEAT. You start to get chilly and uncomfortable and you know it is time to move on.

And that was the end of that day. We hibernated the rest of the day and the comfort of our fortress was greatly appreciated.

11-24-10

We, the three musketeers, reunited—all ailments and injuries put aside. Leigh took the bus from her apartment and we met up in our neighborhood. We then proceeded to Francesco's restaurant and we had a good time. Francesco was chef this day and we had a treat. He is good! We had steak, fried veggies—peppers, eggplant, zucchini and others. Superb. We had artichoke in a pasta with a delightful sauce. The best part was when the owner/chef/ "controller of the thermostat" took the time to talk with us and especially to Leigh. Our new friend became her new contact in the food business in Florence. We had a delightful afternoon with Francesco and finally let him get home to see his wife and four-year-old.

We then proceeded to Fiesole—a promontory overlooking vast parts of Florence to the east. In one glance you can see millions of picture-perfect post cards. Italian cypress, lollipop conifers, olive groves and grapevines. After walking around, we headed back to our fortress and rested. We then drove Leigh to a meeting with Benedetta at her restaurant. After her meeting we headed downtown, put the car in a parking garage and walked to the Duomo. What a massive work of art. What a spellbinding achievement by man. It is without a doubt the most intricate and the most amazing sight I have ever seen. We walked to the Ponte Vechia and enjoyed all of the many many sights. The day came to an end and I was exhausted.

11-25-10

Thanksgiving Day. We are not doing much. Leigh is on a lark for us—searching on the computer to see if somebody is celebrating Thanksgiving in Florence.

2 PM and no word on that. We connect with Leigh only to find out that there are possibilities but they would be quite late—after 9 PM—and Leigh had plans in that time frame with her friends. So we decided to do our own thing. The day wore

AFTERWORD

on and to our delight we had a lengthy conversation with the owner of the fortress about the property. She left books with us and our evening was set exploring the reading material and pictures Federica provided us. If you loved Italy before, you get to love it a lot more after reading about real families and their pursuits and their talents. Federica's grandfather was a renowned artist and many of his licensed masters' reproductions have been sold as originals. We have uncovered the tip of a very large iceberg. Federica and her husband are currently on a fact-finding mission trying to get the bigger picture. Her grandfather's name was Federico Angeli. The book is "Federico And the Angeli Workshop" ISBN 978-88-8347-510-8. www.sillabe.it; info@sillabe.it. We plan to stay in contact with Federica for friendship and updates on her discoveries. Vernon Lee/Violet Paget—writer and activist—previous owner of the house.

11-26-10

Today will be special because tonight we pick up Piera at the train station—really looking forward to it. But today we are going to visit a town called San Gimignano. It is another mountaintop beauty. The ride was beautiful. The weather cooperated and the visual sights of Tuscany are mind-boggling. Everyone takes such care of their property and I am talking hectares/acreage. The landscape looks like the entire horizon to horizon was created by a master—DaVinci! Michelangelo! Our trip almost came to an abrupt end while my right-hand gal, my navigator/keeper of the GPS, screamed out *"Scarpa! Scarpa!"* I was completely caught off guard and almost made a U-turn in the middle of an exit ramp off the autostrada when sanity came back to my brain and I then realized that Ann had only spotted a two-story over-sized SHOE store! I had evil thoughts about my darling wife. Of course, my fright turned to laughter realizing that is my Ann—always expect the unexpected. We climbed the mountainside and arrived at an awesome sight. These towns were built purposely for defensive reasons and the building materials are probably 95% big block stone. All roads are also of large square slats. Now figure out how all of the plumbing and electrical are run! Our plumbers stateside think they have it bad.

We ate at a restaurant that was delightful—old, delicious, eye-candy memorable. Backing up, I failed to mention that, after we got to the top of the mountain the weather situation changed drastically. Between parking the car and walking to the main city gates, the wind became cold and nasty. We trudged on and after entering the city walls we started to feel rain and it began to sting. We were being pelted with hail about the size of bb's. We opened our umbrellas and they were inverted promptly and then you had to correct that problem. The best part was watching Ann correct her umbrella. I wish I'd had a video camera! What we saw and the time we spent was quality time and San Gimignano will be on my list to re-visit. We did have a great meal and we did visit a store or two and a terrific art gallery.

On the way back to Florence Ann recognized some old landmarks and off we went on a side trip. More beauty and farmland with thousands of olive trees and miles of grape vines. We headed back home to prepare to pick up Piera that evening at the train station. We also made plans to pick up Leigh and her roomie, opera singer Tammy, who were taking a bus to our area from *centro storico*. They were actually waiting for us at the neighborhood bar. After quite a bit of confusion and getting to the wrong train station to pick up Piera, she finally arrived. We made a stop at the *pasticeria* for dessert to take to Federicka's for dinner. What an enchanting evening followed!

After dinner we helped take the dishes up to the kitchen where we viewed a 14th-century fresco wall which dated back to Columbus' time. Federica offered to show us a special location in the house. It was the studio her artist grandmother used until she died some eight years before. The room had been left exactly as it was on the last day her grandmother and grandfather painted there. They were rather famous art restorers. It was a magical moment for me and one that I wish I could have shared with my father. He would have been mesmerized by it all. It was a great night.

11-27-10

After a light breakfast at Villa Palmerino we met up with Leigh again and off we went to be tourists in Florence. We did the Duomo again and then went to the outdoor market. I had been whimpering about how much I needed a hat and up to that point I had not found the right one. However, today at a stall in the Florence market I tried on two more hats and the moment I tried on the second one, I knew I had found it! Now with my hat and scarf from two days before I became a distinguished-looking Italian gent!

In our promenade around the market Ann noticed a name on a storefront and realized it was a shop that she had done business with while she had the antique/decorating store on Martha's Vineyard. We went into the shop and Ann spoke with the woman who had been her USA sales representative. Small world.

11-28-10

It was Sunday and our plan was to pick up Leigh for the last time and have lunch at Zibibo's one last time. We all knew it would be hard to say our goodbyes. We three have been like the three musketeers—never offending and always bolstering each other's sense of adventure and adventure after adventure. It has been an experience of a lifetime and I have had the best experience of my life with my three girls.

That particular Sunday was the running of the Florence Marathon. We had heard about it but did not realize how it would affect us. We could not get to Leigh in the city center. Phone call after phone call and attempt after attempt of moving in and around the city meeting police barricades made us abruptly change our plan. It was heartbreaking for all of us. Ann was in tears as she was not going to be able to say goodbye to Leigh in person. Piera tried to console us all. With heavy hearts we left Leigh unceremoniously. I felt like I was leaving part of me behind. I learned to love her more than I thought possible. I was abandoning my daughter. There was nothing else to do but crank in "Torino" in the GPS and off to the north we went.

I haven't said much about Piera other than mention her name. Fact is, she is such a delight and such an easygoing personality that I have totally taken to her and want to kidnap her for Ann and me to always have around as a delightful sidekick. She is the greatest.

Piera had warned that one portion of our trip might be a bit hazardous—going through the mountain range, the Alpines. She was right. The higher we went the more precipitation we encountered. And then—snow. I gripped the steering wheel tightly and slowly a film covered the windshield; I was forced to

AFTERWORD

use the wipers and the washer fluid constantly. Whatever they use on the roads kept kicking up making it very difficult. After what seemed like a decade of driving like that I sensed we were descending in altitude, and the conditions improved greatly. It was a tough trip to say the least. We got to Piera's apartment safely pretty late that evening; somehow Piera whipped up a wonderful meal and then we crashed. Piera gave up her own bed for us and I was grateful.

11-29-10

Today we went to see Piera's mother, Yolanda. We walked to her apartment two blocks away and I realized that Helen and Carmen Patavino had walked these same streets and visited Piera's mother in the same way. Kind of made me feel closer to them. Piera's mother is quite a character even though she was showing advanced old age and mental shortcomings. It did not matter at all. I asked Piera to show me pictures of her family in their prime and I was very pleased that she did that for me.

Then we proceeded downtown to have some lunch. Torino is a beautiful old city with amazing architecture and layouts with a castle and the Italian version of the Eiffel Tower at either end. The main street and all of the buildings were designed to jut out over the very wide sidewalks on both sides of the street. This extends for at least three-quarters of a mile and continues into a broad piazza. The original idea was so that the royal family and entourage would not have to endure strong sun or rain when coming to the piazza.

Piera took us to one of her favorite restaurants in one of these buildings. Quite impressive. I, unfortunately, needed to use the restroom. That was an experience! In the men's room and there on the floor (what looked more like a sink) was the commode—1899 vintage—with foot pedals on either side. One needed to stand on the foot pedals and face forward to do number one. If, on the other hand, number two was necessary, one then needed to turn around backwards and squat down and pray that you don't fall! You get the picture. The ladies declined the need to use the facilities and Piera who had never used them before was now aware. We had another fabulous meal with good conversation and much friendship shared.

The next stop was to visit Tony and Rosetta. Tony is Piera's brother. Unfortunately, Tony is terminally ill with liver cancer. We drove to their apartment and were greeted by two wonderful people. Tony and his girlfriend/partner of many years were anxiously awaiting our arrival. Tony, far from being in any kind of melancholy mood due to his illness, had discovered a bunch of Christmas decorations and toys in a storage space that he hadn't visited in quite a while. When he re-discovered these gems he brought them upstairs and decided to place them around the apartment to make our visit even more cheerful. He is a character of the first order. We laughed and kidded with each other during the entire visit, even though we weren't speaking the same language. I told him, through Piera, when he delivered the baby in his tummy—a big belly at that—insinuating that was the only trouble he was experiencing, he could then visit Ann and me in the US. We laughed.

We were then on our way back home to Piera's to share a final meal before our departure the next day. She even packaged up some small edibles for our travel day. She also had a special surprise for us that she had been waiting to give us—a wedding

AFTERWORD

present. It was a pair of handblown figurines of a man and a woman—clear glass with gold dust incorporated. They were beautiful. How special. We spent the evening looking at old photographs that she had of all of us. With smiles and laughs we ended the day.

11-30-10

We woke with an eye toward the weather report and wondering what it would be like in Milan when we departed. The weather was questionable and therefore we decided to leave Piera early that day eliminating any problems traveling the next day. So after difficult goodbyes, we left after breakfast. So off we went—just the pair of us now on our last leg of a storybook trip and leaving Leigh, Piera, and Italy behind.

We no sooner got on the road when we received a phone call from Piera. "You forgot your wedding present!" It had been in the dining room and we simply forgot it since it was not near our luggage. Piera solved the dilemma by saying that she would now have to bring it to us in the US. That was a good deal!

We arrived at our hotel and snow was falling making us feel very sure that we had made the right decision to leave early. On the prior Sunday we had to make very specific arrangements with Renault-Italy to drop off our car at the airport. Luckily we had been with Piera when the call was made since the Renault gentleman did not speak much English. Piera to the rescue once again. We were to be at Gate 16 Departures at 8:30 AM on December 1st. Without Piera Lord knows the fiasco that could have occurred.

We had a lovely meal at a restaurant in a residential area near the hotel and then it was off to sleep for our last night in Italy.

What would the weather be like tomorrow? Would a little old Italian be at Gate 16 to make us go through a rigorous checkout with the car? Would we get two bottles of the special olive oil through security that we wanted to bring back to the States? Also a bottle of wine and a chunk of pecorino cheese?

12-01-10

We woke to fresh snow sticking to all surfaces, but the roadways were passable. We checked out of the hotel and proceeded to the airport to meet Mr. Renault-Italy at Gate 16. We sloshed through the snow and mush and loaded the car for the final time and were on our way to Malpensa. I am doubting every step of the way that this guy will really be there. We drove slowly because of the conditions and finally arrived at Gate 16. I saw no one. However, I heard Ann say "There he is!" and out of nowhere this guy—old Italian, speaking none or little English—is at the driver-side door. Ann showed him our paperwork and in less than two minutes, he sat in the car and drove off. So much for critical inspection and scrutiny of the car. Later on I thought about the fact that I never asked him for identification. What if he'd just pulled off the perfect theft? Would we be hearing from Renault?

We checked in and then had no problem passing through security. We boarded and had a reasonable flight until we were about to land in New York. We were experiencing wind shear and after circling for a while with no improvement on the field, we were told that we would be landing in Philadelphia to refuel. However, that didn't happen because Philly couldn't handle the customs control for all our passengers. So now what? We needed

AFTERWORD

to fuel up and now the pilots were telling us that the wind had died down in New York. Off we go back to New York. After we landed we went through customs, which was nothing more than the wave of a hand. "Welcome Back to the USA." Because of the delay we missed our connection to Charleston. We wound up booking a flight directly to Charleston with no stopover in Atlanta. Good. That's great, but we have to get to La Guardia to catch that flight. Off to the taxi stand go we. The flight is scheduled to leave at 9:30 PM and we have two hours to get there from Kennedy. When we walked up to the taxi stand there were at least 200 to 300 people waiting in line for a cab. It was cold. It was nasty. And the wind was howling. And, of course, we were not dressed for such weather. We were about to cry. We broke away from the line because there were NO TAXIS in sight. The weather had caused major delays everywhere and caused chaos at Kennedy. No wonder there was overload at the taxi stand. We went back into the terminal and were lucky enough to enlist the help of a very capable and wonderful employee of the Port Authority. He tried to get us transportation to La Guardia. He tried everything, but he finally linked us up with a Port Authority van that would get us to LaGuardia on time for our flight. We were tired. We were totally exhausted and fatigued beyond compare. We took him up on his offer—no matter what the cost.

We arrived at La Guardia and then after still another delay we took off to Charleston. We made it home and thanks to an airport limo we arrived at the house. I really can't remember anything else until I awoke about 2 PM the next day. We now needed major recuperation and time to digest the totally amazing trip we'd experienced.

FROM ITALY AND BACK

ITALY—JUNE 25, 2012 TO JULY 23, 2012

25TH OF JUNE 2012

Start of our next adventure. Ann and I are in an Army lodge in Maryland—to be specific, the Lodge at Fort George Meade. Yes, a pleasant stay—BUT! Before the day is out we will be flying back to Jacksonville, Florida. Seems that we are discovering the summer months flood the *Space A* travel program with troops on R&R and military movements plus military families on vacation. Let me catch up to myself. When a Navy man starts telling a story, you can tell if it is a lie when he starts out "Once Upon a Time" or "This Ain't No Bullshit!" This story starts out more like "Once Upon a Bull Shit."

Ann and I had made our way back to Sarasota, Florida, from Martha's Vineyard to square away any loose ends before we departed for out first "Space A" travel experience from the Naval Air Station in Jacksonville, Forida. I have to mention that all during our stay on Martha's Vineyard the weather was horrible. We didn't have one decent day there. And rain followed us all the way to Sarasota and accelerated as we got there. Four days of torrential downpour culminating with our last day in Sarasota without POWER! We managed to get our act together and with mail and bank and other household duties taken care of (amidst more rain), we were able to leave and off we go. Of course, it rained and rained hard for most of the trip to Jacksonville.

Our plan was to arrive a day early, stay at the Navy Lodge, and be rested for the next day's activity. We had an early dinner at Mulligan's, the restaurant on the base golf course. We

AFTERWORD

sat on the verandah overlooking the golf course and it was all a delight, especially when we met another couple who were traveling "Space A," and we compared stories. I should back up and explain what "Space A" is all about. When you retire from active duty from the military, you qualify to fly on most military aircraft that fly between most of the military bases in the USA and throughout the world. That is wonderful—but—it is a hit-or-miss proposition. You move in the system only if there is room available and you may not be able to return to your departure location. Hit or Miss! To the experienced "Space A" person you plan your trip in reverse and hope for the best. It's a wonderful benefit, but one must be flexible and patient. We understood that. But we were not prepared for what we were to encounter.

After a restful night the real adventure was to begin. Arranging for long-term parking for our car was an adventure in itself, but once that was done we were off to the passenger terminal to await the first leg of our trip from Jacksonville to BWI (Baltimore International Airport.) From there we were expecting to fly to Ramstein, Germany, and then on to Aviano, Italy. While waiting at the terminal Ann discovered that our "Space A" registration for our flight out of BWI was about to expire one day short of our departure. Panic set in. After many attempts to get that done from where we were, we learned that we would have to do that at the BWI terminal. More unknowns.

Our plane finally landed. It came in from GITMO (Guantanamo Bay, Cuba). It's raining—hard. Passengers disembarking are wet, wet, wet. The rain stopped for a bit and when the plane was ready for boarding the sky opened up again and it started pouring, so much so that they used a shuttle van to get passengers from the terminal to the plane—a very short distance.

The flight was uneventful, but we were anxious to get to the desk at BWI to straighten out our registration. We landed and found the desk and learned that none of it mattered because we weren't going to get on a plane to Ramstein—no way. This was summer and our category 6 status would never get us on board. Oh, boy. We need to come up with a plan B. We were able to get a reservation for the night at Fort Meade and had some re-thinking to do and some fancy footwork to see if we could get ourselves back to Jacksonville in time to connect with a flight to Sigonella, Sicily on Saturday that we had learned about while waiting at the terminal. Luck was with us and we secured a commercial flight for only $80 and we would be back in Jacksonville in plenty of time to make that flight. We stayed at the Clarion Hotel near the airport and actually spent a very pleasant two days just sitting at their pool and enjoying meals there. We arranged for a cab to pick us up on Saturday morning and our lady driver was a cross between Annie Oakley and Phyllis Diller. What a character and what a ride! After hugging and kissing and saying goodbye, she dropped us once again at the terminal and she was off—only to realize a short while later that we'd left the computer in the cab! After a good deal of turmoil and some anxious moments we were able to connect with her and she headed back to the terminal with our computer safe in her hands. Phew.

While waiting for our flight several other "Space A" travelers appear and we schmooze and gobble up all of their wisdom and share personal details. We became a small family with a common

AFTERWORD

goal—Sigonella, Sicily. After a whole lot more anxiety—and more rain—we are ready to board. By the time we did board we were soaked to the skin. Oh, well, we are leaving! The plane was great—a Boeing 737—beautiful and spacious and just seven of us on board. We re-fueled in the Azores and next stop was Sigonella on Sunday morning when base activity slowed to a snail's pace. We waited for two hours for a shuttle bus and realized that the base is split in two—seven miles apart from one another. We are hot. We are tired. We are hungry. Did I mention that we are really really tired? It took several hours to figure out what we could do and we even walked a mile one way down the road to see if there was lodging at NAS I instead of having to get to NAS II and get a room at the Navy Lodge. Finally we were able to rent a car and move on to NAS II. Following directions I made a wrong turn at an intersection, and oh what a mistake! It turned out to be a country lane noted for hookers on the roadside every quarter of a mile or so. We backtracked to our original point of departure and more clarification of the directions from the gate guard at NAS I. When I told the guard my hooker-lane story he knew all about it and smiled. And off we went to NAS I, the neatest, newest base with amenities galore. Finally. We were in heaven and we could rest. After a much-needed shower I kissed my wife and lay down for a nap. A long nap.

    Feeling much better we drove off to the Navy Exchange and explored the base a little. We heard some music and saw crowds gathering—an early start to celebrating the Fourth of July perhaps. A full stage show was in progress with food tents, face painting and a lot of smiling faces. We walked among the crowd and we were amazed at the location. It was called Mid-Town and it duplicated a lot of new towns in the USA making all service personnel and their dependents feel like there was a little bit of their hometown here in Sigonella.

After this wonderful experience we wanted to sit down and have a nice meal, so off we went just outside the gate. There were about six or seven shaky-looking joints directly across the street. The façades all look a little questionable, but when you open the door everything was quite different. We made the right choice and arrived at a beautiful patio just through the doorway. Our waiter was Ezio and we enjoyed a meal that was delicious as well as eye appealing. At a nearby table sat a number of obvious US Naval personnel and Marines. They were a frisky group and some foul language slipped out and continued to increase as the drinks flowed. A few of the guys looked over at us and attempted to apologize, but I told them that it wasn't foul at all—it was just a form of grammar accentuating a point. "In fact," I told them, "I was having a fucking pretty good time!" Nothing vulgar about making a strong point. As soon as they heard me say the "f" word, we were friends forever and each member of their entourage made their way over to our table to mingle with us. As soon as they realized that I was a twenty-three year vet from the nuclear submarine Navy with a lot of accumulated submerged time, they elevated me to a very high position in their minds. After many laughs, many hugs and kisses we established a connection that will last a long time. Emails were exchanged. Picture a burly rather muscular dude with a bikini top and his own bathing suit and swim goggles on, making muscle-man moves. This was Mikey. In a restaurant no less. We old folks had to call it a day and these guys partied on until the restaurant closed.

AFTERWORD

The next day we wound up near the Sigonella Inn—a very nice hotel with a restaurant and gorgeous huge swimming pool with a wet bar. We approached the parking area and noticed one of the lovely young ladies we'd met the night before and she told us that her crowd was all there. We found a parking space and made our way back to the restaurant passing the pool. We ordered our food and I went back to the pool and here came Mikey. I stood in his path until he spotted me and then more hugs and kisses followed. He wanted to see the pretty lady—Ann! I led him to her and he blushed and gushed about how pretty Ann was and kissed her hand in a loving way. After our meal we went back to our room and rested for the remainder of the afternoon preparing for the Italian vs. Spain soccer Euro Cup extravaganza.

The next morning we had to get up early to take the car back to the rental office location. I haven't mentioned how bloody hot it was during this time. After dropping the car off we decided to walk to the Gateway Lodge, another hotel accommodation on NAS II. We walked and we walked and we walked. Maybe the heat had something to do with it, but it seemed to take forever—and we were dragging our luggage too. We sat in the lobby for a respite and to get up our courage to make our way back to the terminal and sign up for our return flight to the States. That done we had to kill some time waiting for the shuttle bus back to NAS I. A little chai tea and a lackluster sandwich was enjoyed al fresco and then it was shuttle time. We arrived back at the lodge and we decided to stay in our room to watch Wimbledon matches as we waited for our taxi to take us to the Catania airport. Every moment became an adventure and we had so much fun every step of the way and making new friends every day. The night before we arrived back at the lodge, there was a woman attending the front desk. We had noticed her a few times but had never struck up a conversation. This time was different. We made fast friends with Marilyn Lazzara—born in Brooklyn, New York to Sicilian parents—and offered schooling as a young girl at a nunnery either in the US or in Sicily. She chose Sicily, married, had two children, and never went back to the US. She was fun. We laughed and we are friends for life. In our conversation we learned that Marilyn has a friend by the last name of Piccolo. My cousin, Brian Piccolo's father was born in Sicily, so I became convinced that her friend is related to my relatives!

After a strange and somewhat crazy trip we finally arrived in Bari to behold the most beautiful smile of one Leigh Vincola and we were off in Leigh's car to her new home in Ostuni—*La Cita Bianca*—the White City. The approach even at night was magnificent—the roads a little tight, the hilly streets a little steep. We arrived at Leigh's apartment and we were amazed to be living for this period of time in a museum of ancient construction. I could not figure how these artisans could pile stones in intricate patterns to achieve stairs, rooms, and floors. We chatted for a while and then went off to have a bite to eat. In Italy even though it is past 11 PM, the town comes alive. We ate and drank until it was time for a little "*passigiata*" through a beautiful park. It was past 1 am and children and adults of all ages are out and about.

The next day we awoke after 10 AM and after attempting to get electronic devices working, we were off to have lunch.

AFTERWORD

Leigh took us to an old olive oil pressing factory completely carved into a stone cliff under the old walls of the city—one of her favorites. Impressive!! The owner took us for a tour—totally mind-boggling—room after room made out of solid stone. We were able to see how the olive presses worked in days of old. At its time it was the marvel of primitive efficiency.

WEDNESDAY, JULY 4, 2012

We packed up our beach bags and off we went to a very unusual beach—a stretch of solid rock and a lovely little swimming area. We had a wonderful time there. The Adriatic Sea seems to be extremely salty and to my taste buds, a delightful taste at that.

Off we go back to the "Villa Leigh." Did I tell you about her crazy neighbor who walks about and in a high-pitched Louis Armstrong kind of voice, rants and raves at anyone available? After he has his say he abruptly stops and walks away, not looking any worse for wear. We shower and rest the hot afternoon away.

When we are revived and the cool evening approaches—and amazingly it does cool off to a most delightful temperature—we socialize among ourselves some more with more laughs and reflection about our day and our adventures.

THURSDAY, JULY 5, 2012

Today Leigh took us on a marvelous culinary adventure somewhere on the coast of the Adriatic uncluttered by condos and mega-mansions. We made our way to a dusty sandy driveway ending in a parking lot completely covered in netting—the same type farmers use to place on the ground under their olive trees to capture their harvest after shaking the branches vigorously.

The purpose of the netting is to shade the cars while you are enjoying your meal. The meal consisted of mouth-watering fresh fish. Sitting on a veranda overlooking the Adriatic, waves gently touching shore, we ate squid, shrimp, mussels, and the most delightful of all—octopus. It is almost impossible to describe the flavor of the octopus; it was almost a God-like experience! Cheese, olives, beer and wine accompanied the meal, and, of course, delicious bread. My mouth is watering just re-visiting this memory. We did finally leave after spending several hours just taking it all in and pleasing every sense—sight, sound, touch, and best of all TASTE. I remember walking to the car having this overpowering feeling of contentment and relaxation. I wanted to find a hammock and complete the orgasm of eating indulgence and pleasure.

A couple of kilometers north of our fantastic meal, we stopped to have our "*cappuccino frio*"—cappuccino with ice cream in it. This is not something you can find just anywhere, so it is a sublime treat. This drink was sensory experience #99 of this day and it came at the best time. The caffeine in the drink took me from complete drowsy exhaustion to being wide-awake and raring to go.

The day was only half over as we proceeded back to the house and freshened up because we had an appointment to meet with Leigh's friend, a real estate agent, whom she met while filming for House Hunters International. Ann and I are going to see what is available in the surrounding area. We met Giovanni at his office and then off we went in his car on still another, what—ADVENTURE. After a ride exiting the city of Ostuni, we headed out into the countryside and the drive was

AFTERWORD

delightful and pleasing. We approached our first stop and my attitude was going to be "keep it cool; don't over react if you see something that pleases you." We pulled off the main road and see a walled drive and a gate into the property. Even before the gate is opened I blurt out "I love it!" I'm blown away with visual pleasures. How about thick stone wall, roof entirely of stone and masonry, stone arches, tremendous portico, etc. etc. And how about olive trees, fig trees, almond trees, and also walnut trees. There is also a small *trullo* storage building and cistern and the view is gorgeous. The interior was great, too—we truly loved it and could definitely see ourselves in it. We saw two other properties but nothing compared to this.

We met Leigh at the Pink Lady to tell her about what we saw and we acted like newlyweds shopping for our first home.

We called it a day to recharge our batteries.

FRIDAY, JULY 6, 2012

After a good night's sleep we are heading to the beach again. This time we are going to a cabana beach. We rent an umbrella and three chaise chairs. An attendant loads up a dolly and we pick a spot. He drills a hole in the sand with a manual auger, sets it, opens it and all of the sturdy chaise chairs and departs. We are good for the day. We ate a light lunch at the beach, not wanting to spoil our planned birthday celebration for Leigh at the elegant Masseria called Il Frantoio. It was a wonderful day at the beach.

After resting at home for a bit we were ready to depart for Leigh's birthday treat. We drove through a region of thousands of ancient olive trees and many hectares of agriculture. We proceeded up a fieldstone-walled drive and eventually arrived at the beautiful sight before us. I have to use the word "beautiful" once again because I do not know another word to better describe what we have flooded our brains with. A *masseria* is a self-contained walled compound containing a chapel, wheat- and food-storage buildings and in a cave beneath the *masseria* is a full factory devoted to olive-oil production. Leigh had been here several times before through her work with Southern Visions, so she knew how spectacular it was. We even had a tour of the entire property and learned that they grow a lot of the foods used in the kitchen. The dinner was fabulous and the atmosphere was like no other. No wonder Leigh chose that spot for her birthday. It is a must for any traveler in the region.

SATURDAY JULY 7, 2012

After a lazy morning we set off to experience the Ostuni town market. It seemed modest and unassuming at first. At the very first stand we approached Leigh was met with shouts of joy and warm greetings. They were the cheese vendors and they had become friends because they too, were in the House Hunters film with Leigh the week before we got there. The guys were so much fun. They had us try so much cheese and we even took pictures with them. After making our purchases and moving on, the full capacity of this market was revealed. There were two full streets filled with food vendors—fruit to meat and all that could be imagined. Beyond that were clothing vendors and it just went on and on. We stopped to have some lemon ice and watched the man scrape the ice. I was like a little kid remembering how much I loved it.

AFTERWORD

We went back home to rest again and then left Leigh for a while so she could get some work done and we went to the Pink Lady to watch "Wimbledon." We loved hanging out at the Pink Lady and we were so happy that we could get to watch our tennis too.

We decided to drive Leigh by the house we saw with Giovanni and somehow the gate was mysteriously unlocked so we were able to walk around the entire property. Leigh loved it too. We can dream, can't we?

Our next adventure was to see "Gelso Bianco" the cooking school that was recently built and part of Southern Visions as well. We got to see the whole property that is really amazing and then we walked through the town of Alberobello, the town where the *trulli* abound. It was wonderful.

SUNDAY, JULY 8, 2012

We spent the morning lollygagging around, talked, read, and stayed out of the heat of the day. After lying down for a bit of a rest, Ann and I strolled to our little island of contact with the outside world—the Pink Lady—again. It became our go-to place, and yes, we were going to be able to see the Wimbledon finals between Roger Federer and Andy Murray. We chatted with other people in the place—Americans who had reconnected and married like us—and lots of Brits who were very interested in seeing Andy Murray win the championship. We, of course, are avid Roger Federer fans. We were there the whole time with a woman from England, who was rooting for Andy rather vigorously, only for us to find out later that she was Leigh's colleague's mother. It turned out to be rather humorous.

We wound up having dinner later with the entire British crew and we had a ball. We sat in the square and laughed and talked with these wonderful people. Leigh has some great friends here in Ostuni.

JULY 10, 2012

We are off on a mission. Ann and I are being driven to Monopoli, a neat town with a sheltered harbor and the town where Leigh first lived when she came south to look for Southern Visions after leaving Florence. Of course we had to see a little bit of Southern Visions' location (where all the bikes are kept) and then we got down to serious matters—eating! Leigh took us to a place just off the water. I don't remember what the ladies had chosen because my choice—fish spaghetti—was so very good that I became silent and I was brought to prayer eating every morsel. Another great—no another excellent—wait a minute—it was another wonderful experience!

After the meal we walked a bit, but it was short because of the heat. We did manage to go by Leigh's old apartment; a number of her old neighbors spotted her and it was fun for her to reconnect with them. They remembered one specific vision that they thought was weird—Leigh doing yoga on her balcony. They thought it was strange.

We ventured back home to rest up because later that evening we were going to the airport in Brindisi to pick up cousin Piera, who was flying in from Torino. We hadn't seen Piera in two years and we were all excited to see her again.

After a somewhat difficult time on the road getting to the airport we finally had Piera within our sights. With much glee and smiles and hugs and kisses we headed back to Ostuni and had a meal at the local *pescatoria*. It was fabulous having Piera back with us.

JULY 11, 2012

Our next plan was to drive south toward Lecce. After packing and more chatter we headed out to find the *masseria* that we had booked through Airbnb. Our destination is in the town of Martano. After a bit we found our spot and were pleased at the warm and friendly welcome we received. It was a great spot, but the best part was that it had a pool! It was HOT in Italy at the time especially being so far south.

We went into the town after checking in and had another fantastic meal and wonderful experience and then back to the pool. We loved it. The temperature of the water was perfect. We were in heaven.

After resting a bit we went into the city of Lecce. It is the largest city in the south, full of Baroque influence and beauty and elegance. Our visit included a wine-bar stop and we noshed on some appetizers—olives, bread, fennel, carrots. Tired and thrilled about our journey we headed back to Martano.

After rising the next morning the pool was on everyone's mind and we did take advantage of it for hours. We had a lovely breakfast earlier with our hosts, which included fruit, biscuits, yogurt, pastries and cappuccino. Then we went back to the restaurant from yesterday so that I could have my lasagna that I had asked for the day before. Well, it was certainly worth it.

That evening we were off to a little town called Colignano where a "*Sagra*" was taking place that night. This is something Leigh had heard about and wanted to experience. The town is charming with a castle and full of Italian charm. The Sagra is a town event featuring food tasting and lots of fun. You buy a sheet of tickets and get a map and a wine glass in a convenient pouch. We jumped into the middle of it and we all four took turns figuring out the lay out. It was made challenging because the sites were all over town, not just around the park. We persevered and did ourselves proud finding enough of the tents to fill our bellies to full. At one point I started realizing the heat and the wine were taking a toll on me, so I quickly switched to plenty of water and no more wine! The evening was salvaged and another WONDERFUL time—tired, stuffed and ready to lie down. Back to the *masseria*.

Our final morning at the *masseria* was highlighted by a lengthy and in-depth conversation about the history of the property. Having Piera with us provides us the native Italian to understand and interpret it all. Time to say *arrivederci*.

We decided to take the scenic route back to Ostuni and drove up the coast. We saw beautiful towns with rocky ledges and cliffs down to the water where people swam in the beautiful blue/green waters. We stopped for lunch and had another Italian experience with Piera and for the first time we were not impressed by the meal we had! She surely let them know.

We were killing time before we had to take Piera to the airport and that meant we would be losing one of our fun-seekers. Too soon we were at the airport and as quickly as it started, it was ending and we had to say goodbye.

JULY 14, 2012

Another visit to the Saturday market. This time Ann and I ventured out by ourselves leaving Leigh to get some work accomplished. We couldn't believe the size of the whole thing. It is almost three acres. We picked up a few things that Leigh needed and we enjoyed strolling through the maze of tents with everything under the sun for sale. At home again Leigh put together a fabulous lunch of orrechieto and tomatoes and a special local cheese. It was soooooo good. And fresh peaches for dessert.

Leigh had some work-related stuff to do and we managed to just spend another afternoon enjoying our surroundings and feeling very lucky to be where we were. I also managed to fix Leigh's grill up on her roof deck.

Ann began discovering that our flight back to Jacksonville had been changed and we might be experiencing some uncertainty about our trip home. Ah well, we knew that might be the case. We'll deal with it.

That evening we went to the *pescatoria* again which became another thing altogether. The wait was very long to get a table and they actually had to place another table under a tree far away from the other customers and umbrellas. After a while we felt fine about it and we realized we were in a good spot. At this place you order your meal from the fish you can look at inside and then it is served to you outside. Delicious.

All right, we head home and have a nice walk back and relax for a while and in due time Leigh arrives home and we hear about her afternoon and evening in more detail when she settled some new guests in. It was very nice to confirm that she had a great encounter and made new friends. It was off to bed for us.

It felt so good to be in the horizontal position with our minds somewhat into a relaxed mode instead of "What's next?—let's get going—let's have the next experience!" Upon awakening, Ann began checking emails again still concerned about our flight home. She discovered that we had a good contact and friend in Marilyn Lazzara at the Navy Lodge in Sigonella who could be of great help. Our path became a little clearer and our resolve more positive.

Leigh planned to sleep in. She has exhausted herself entertaining us, driving us, and maintaining her own work schedule. She has done it admirably. Today's plan was to drive to a town called Cisternino, which Leigh has raved about and we, of course, wish to experience all that the town could present. We had a light lunch consisting of three different types of olives, mozzarella, hard cheese called *chicacalda*, arugula, and some fine Italian beer called Drecher—full bodied.

Ann has started packing and we have to face the fact—our stay is coming to an end. We lazed away the day and then headed on to Cisternino for our 8 PM dinner—Italian style. As we approached the old town, the white stone, ancient architecture and beautiful people mesmerized us. In the main piazza a bandstand had been erected and most of the band members were tweaking their audio and warming up their instruments.

After Leigh dropped us off and then went to park the car we all did a little shopping and walking around the enchanting town. And I did a lot of architectural viewing—thinking of my dad all the time. How I would love to have him here with me. He taught me more about architecture than anyone. My dad, my dad, my dad—the Renaissance man. After walking around some more enjoying the narrow streets with beautiful flowers cascading from balconies, we settled on a restaurant for our

AFTERWORD

dinner—Bere Vecchie. The service was superb, the location was superb, the drinks were superb, and the food was super superb. After finishing our meal Leigh had a shot of a drink called Aro. It is a bittersweet drink that is supposed to aid digestion. To me that's a bit of a stretch, sort of like taking of shot of white lightning! I had a café and I am getting closer to adding this to my Dr. Pepper routine. It does pick you up without the caffeine jitters that regular coffee often creates. (It's like the Italian wine—no headaches!)

Show time and the band was in full swing. We wandered through the winding streets to come out on the main piazza again and now the square was packed with people. We were in for a major treat. Were they good? No, no, they were GREAT! We stood until some seats became available and the enjoyment only intensified with our newfound level of physical comfort. And they continued—song after song—no breaks. In the lengthy Italian introduction to each new song, there were always English words sprinkled throughout and you had no difficulty recognizing what they would be playing. They were top-notch musicians. And then a female singer began and she was even better! We actually got to speak with her when the band did finally take a break and learned that she had been to the States and had entertained there too. We collected her business card.

After leaving Cisternino we returned to Ostuni to meet up with Leigh's friends again in the big piazza. What a night! It was kind of our going-away party. Leigh seemed to have planned the perfect night for us with the band in Cisternino and all of her great friends in the piazza. What a girl! Our girl LEIGH! After lots of hugs and kisses and promises to come back we strolled home for the last time. It was after 1 am and we were leaving the next day.

We weren't flying out till 9:30 PM from Bari to Catania, Sicily, so we spent the day helping Leigh get our room and her little house in good order for the Airbnb guests who would be arriving shortly. We completed our packing, loaded the car, and began making our way toward Bari, but we decided to make one more stop in a small town on the way—Polagno de Mare, the home of singer Domenico Modugno of "Volare" fame. It is a spectacular sight. The visit was capped off with the best gelato I have ever had.

We arrived at the Bari Aeroporto and the sad moment of having to say goodbye was upon us. There are no words to express how hard it was to try to tell Leigh how much of a great time we had and how, because of her effort, the time we shared together was precious and special. Soon her car was on its way to start her next chapter, and it will be another interesting chapter indeed.

Leigh is to be admired and praised for who she is and how strong she is to make it in a foreign country. She has friends, but she is operating her life single-handedly—by herself. Her support mechanism comes from within her amazing strength and from afar from her mom and me. We are committed to be there for her whenever we are needed.

After a little delay we were in the air. We had made arrangements beforehand to have a taxi pick us up, but with the delay we weren't sure what to expect when we landed. We landed, picked up our bags, walked through the exit, and there is Rosario with a sign in hand—VOTTA'S. I could kiss him. We had used his service a couple of times and he was a gem. Our trip to NAV I

AFTERWORD

and the Navy Lodge on the Sigonella base went by quickly with Rosario telling us one story after another about taxi nightmares. He entertained us for the whole trip.

We arrived at the Lodge tired and full of questions about our flight. Will we be out in a matter of days, or would it be longer? Calls were made with no good answers coming back. We learned that there is a broken plane that is now in Athens, Greece. This is supposed to be our plane to take us back to Jacksonville, FL. We went to bed and we started calling again as soon as we woke up the next day. The information available was so confusing. I actually got to speak with the detachment commander, but he didn't know much either. The terminal didn't know anything either. We just kept hearing, "Call back tomorrow." We couldn't do anything else but wait. We calmed down a bit and decided to go over to the beautiful huge pool at the Sigonella Inn across the road. It is a lovely spot and we were in seventh heaven for a little while.

As the sun went down we went back to our room at the Lodge and made some more phone calls. Still nothing. We were told to call again tomorrow at 8:30 am. We decided to walk over to the restaurant we had been to at the beginning of our trip where we'd met Mikey and his gang. No Mikey, but Ezio the waiter we'd met before was there. Our meal was another knockout—spaghetti with mussels. During the meal a group of men entered and they told Ezio they would be either four or seven in all. My ears perked up and when they were deciding what to order, I blurted out "Try the mussels and spaghetti." They appreciated the suggestion.

While they were enjoying their meal and talking among themselves, I sort of heard words like "repair," "part needed," "delay," "Athens." Could this be??? The plane is repaired and may be here in Sigonella? Is this the flight crew? I tell Ann this may be the answer we have been looking for. I excused myself and boldly asked the table of potential joy to us—"Are you the crew of the C-40 (737) that was broken down in Athens, Greece?" The answer is yes! The aircraft is parked on the tarmac nearby at NAV II. Ann then asked—"Will you be taking passengers?" The men at the table point to the pilot and he says, "Yes." "When is departure time?" And he said, "Be there at 1100 hours." How ecstatic could two people be? All of our phone calls provided no answers, but here we were seven miles away from the airport in an Italian restaurant and we have solved our dilemma. We missed a plane on Sunday that was originally scheduled for Tuesday, and the plane delay allowed us to catch up with it. There is a God! We contacted Rosario again and he will pick us up and get us to the airport tomorrow morning.

We called the terminal again at 8:30 AM just to make sure the information that we got the night before was correct. It was a tough few days of uncertainty. Sure enough—Roll Call 11:00 AM. All is right with the universe. Rosario delivered us promptly and last-minute checks at the desk confirm we were valid and registered. We even met some friends who were on the incoming flight with us. There were smiles and hugs and confirmation that we all had had a good time in Italia. Upon boarding we realized that half of the plane was rigged for cargo. This meant that there were a limited number of available seats. There was a large number of military active-duty types and we wondered whether our "Space A" availability would be jeopardized. Upon entering the plane we were greeted by all of the military types and in the first row we met Allison, Mikey's girlfriend. We felt at home. The flight wasn't as luxurious as our flight in, but we were on it and we were on our way home.

Ann's anxieties began stirring again as to what would await us in Jacksonville when we arrived. Would there be room at the Lodge? Will we be able to get our car out of storage? The answer is—It is what it is and will be what it will be.

Well, it was all fine. And we got home. When are we going back?

About the Author

After an extensive career as an educator, consultant, and business owner, Ann Votta is now concentrating on memoir and travel writing. Her background includes fifteen years as a Professor of Early Childhood Education, twenty years as a nationally recognized human resource and work/life consultant, and ten years in retail as owner of an antiques and interiors business on Martha's Vineyard. She lives in Sarasota, Florida with her husband Alan.

www.ingramcontent.com/pod-product-compliance
Lightning Source LLC
Chambersburg PA
CBHW052022290426
44112CB00014B/2333